WELCOME TO THE WISDOM OF THE WORLD

Welcome to the Wisdom of the World

And Its Meaning for You

JOAN CHITTISTER

William B. Eerdmans Publishing Company

Grand Rapids, Michigan / Cambridge, U.K.

Published 2007 by

Wm. B. Eerdmans Publishing Co.

2140 Oak Industrial Drive N.E., Grand Rapids, Michigan 49505 /

P.O. Box 163, Cambridge CB3 9PU U.K.

Printed in the United States of America

12 11 10 09 08 07   7 6 5 4 3 2 1

Library of Congress Cataloging-in-Publication Data

Chittister, Joan.
  Welcome to the wisdom of the world and its meaning for you /
  Joan D. Chittister.
    p.   cm.
  ISBN 978-0-8028-2894-1 (cloth: alk.paper)
  1. Religions.   I. Title

 BL80.3.C45   2007
 200 — dc22
 2007009964

www.eerdmans.com

*This book is dedicated, with great respect,
to the members of the International Committee for the Peace Council
and to Daniel Gomez-Ibanez, Executive Director,
who together model a common and universal wisdom.*

*It is especially intended to recognize Samdech Preah Maha Ghosananda,
the late, past Supreme Patriarch of Cambodian Buddhism, whose
dharma walks through the minefields of Cambodia go on giving
life to the wisdom this world needs and this book honors.*

Contents

Acknowledgments

Writing is a literary exercise, of course, but only at one level. At its best, writing makes thought possible, accessible, readable, and clear. Those additional dimensions of the writer's task are a process that engage the wisdom, the skills, and the background of far more minds than that of the writer alone. I consider myself particularly blessed by the number of people who have been willing to participate in this particular project. They have brought to this work considerable breadth of theological knowledge as well as historical experience. They have made the rough edges smooth.

I am always grateful for this kind of collaboration. In fact, I would be bereft without it.

Where this material and presentation of content is concerned I acknowledge with special gratitude the responses of my own Benedictine Sisters. Sisters Marlene Bertke, Susan Doubet, Carolyn Gorny-Kopkowski, Mary Lou Kownacki, Anne McCarthy, Mary Ellen Plumb, Ellen Porter, Linda Romey, Marilyn Schauble, and Charlotte Zalot brought a wide range of professional, spiritual, theological, historical, and editorial experience that gave both depth and clarity to this work.

Jeremy Langford, writer and publisher in his own right, gave the manuscript a special kind of scrutiny both for content and quality. Dr. Gail Grossman Freyne examined the work for its psycho-social dimensions with her usual carefulness. Professor Amy-Jill Levine, Rabbi Sandy Sasso,

Imam Feisal Abdul Rauf, and Professor Sean Freyne, director of the Center for Interfaith Studies, Trinity College, Dublin, have been particularly generous in bringing light to the concepts that underlie and link the traditions. I am immensely grateful to these people who have worked in these areas all their lives for their willingness to broaden my understanding of all these great faiths. Just knowing them has been an education for me.

Sandra DeGroot, my editor at Eerdmans, brought great heart and continued encouragement to the project. Earlier than most, she sensed the need for a work such as this in an integrated but tumultuous world.

The space and time to work on so broad and so reflective a study is no small part of its creation. For that gift of time and distance I am grateful without measure to Gail and Sean Freyne, to William and Elizabeth Vorsheck.

Finally, I am grateful to Sister Maureen Tobin, long-time assistant and friend, whose organization, support, and sensitivity to every aspect of the work have done more to bring this book to light than words can ever say.

There is no way to thank all of these contributors to this compendium of human wisdom other than to say that their own wisdom is very much alive in it. Without them, in fact, it simply would not be.

Answers from the Ages

Are people really unique? Is there anything in the human condition that is peculiar to ourselves alone as a people? Have any other peoples ever gone through the things we are going through now? Answer: it all depends on what you're talking about.

Yes, we are unique as a people. We live in a different time than those before us. We are inheritors of a specific culture. And yes, every culture is peculiar to its own time. What shapes us as a people today, or touches our lives, or challenges our souls is different than it must have been a century ago.

And yet, at the same time, other peoples have gone through the very things we are going through right now, because, whatever the distinctions of time, place, and culture, whatever the time and place in which we have lived, we are all human beings — just human beings, wherever and whenever we live, subject to the same emotional limits, dealing with the same range of emotional responses.

We have something in common, then, with all people who have ever lived in any place or era anywhere. And all of these peoples have grappled with the same kinds of questions and have arrived at their own answers. We have at our fingertips, then, a reservoir of wisdom as broad as the sky, as deep as history.

This book is meant to explore how those other cultures, other peoples

— long before us and apparently completely unlike us — have answered the same kinds of life questions that plague us now. It is meant to help us profit from the wisdom of those who in other ages and traditions grappled with the same kinds of human concerns we have now — only differently.

The concerns with which the book deals do not come from theology books or philosophical musings. They come from average people, who, in reaching out to find some kind of solace or direction in their own lives, have identified whole categories of concern that, over time, touch us all. And they have done it in the simplest, commonest way: in letters.

One of the most distant and, at the same time, one of the most intimate pieces of literature in the modern world is the ordinary, everyday, personal letter. Today, for the first time in history, people can sit almost anywhere and at the touch of a button contact almost anyone in the world. They can pour out their hearts, vent their angers, beg for help, engage in deep philosophical reflection, and tell the most personal details of their lives. Most of all, encouraged by empathy, protected by the anonymity that computers afford, they can do it without ever having to look another person directly in the eye. They can talk to the other as if to themselves.

I know because I get a lot of that. They sit in the dark and ask questions. I sit in the dark and write back.

Over the years, as a result, the letters that have come in every day have accumulated by the thousands. I read all of them and, barring lost files or illegible addresses or bad email transmissions, I have made an effort to respond to each and every one of them. After all, people say very important things when they write to people they do not know but think may be willing to listen. The anonymity of both the writer and the reader allows for a great deal of candor, even a good deal of emotion.

It has never been easy to keep up with that amount of mail, but it has been worth it. Reading those letters has been for me an exercise in humanity that far outstripped anything sociological surveys or human development textbooks or philosophy lectures ever managed to teach me.

I answer the letters, yes — at least at one level — but not really. Underlying all the data, all the frustration or the fear, are questions too real, too raw, too deep, certainly too obliquely expressed to pursue at length in an email. A one-line response to the great questions of life belies the real meaning of them to us all. No, these questions are far *too* valuable for that kind of treatment.

It is those issues, those questions — the questions and issues that plague my readers and fill my mail — with which this book deals. But it is about far more than that as well. It is also about the way other people, in other ages, other cultures, other spiritual traditions, have dealt with these subjects. Not in our words, perhaps, or with our images, maybe, but definitely with our concerns.

These questions touch on what it is to be a real human being, a really spiritual person. They deserve more than a thirty-word gossip column response. They deserve a lifetime of reflection from us all. And so they are the subject matter of this book.

Issues such as these are far beyond the particular circumstances of a particular person. Instead, they trace the contours of the human condition. They track the movement of the soul from dailiness to death with an eye to strengthening its spiritual fiber in the midst of stress. Sooner or later every one of us is required to face issues such as these in our own lives. They beg for reflection. They insist that we grapple with them. They require us to resolve them — one way or another — in our own lives. And, eventually, everybody does, somehow.

The final proof of the value of these issues may lie in the fact that they are not simply cultural — meaning that they are not simply important to this time and place and this people or person. These issues are universal. There is no culture that has not contended with them, no spiritual tradition that has not grappled with them. Perhaps that is exactly why they are so important. Perhaps that is the clue that they are, at base, really unanswerable, at least definitively. And yet every great spiritual tradition tries.

The very fact that there is no major value system that does not, in some way, deal with these very issues may be the best measure we have of what it really means to grow up spiritually. The implication is that to become holy we must all go through these maturation points in life. We all need to seek enlightenment about how to live well, to live vibrantly, as we go. In the face of everything life has to offer, to become one with the universe each of us must share in its confusions and work through its conundrums to the point of spiritual maturity.

Each great spiritual tradition, in its own way, suggests a model of what it means to be a holy person. Each of them shines a light on the human ideal. Each of them talks about what it takes to grow, to endure, to develop, to live a spiritual life in a world calculatingly material and sometimes maddeningly unclear.

Yet, most of the responses to these great life questions do not come from catechetical manuals or theological treatises. In each of the traditions, we find the kind of wisdom literature that transcends both spiritual techniques and sacred theory. This kind of wisdom literature sets out simply to illuminate those passing moments in life that too often seem to be transitory, even worthless, but in which, underneath it all, some of the most disturbing, most challenging personal themes of life — ambition, success, security, exhilaration, endurance, romance, abandonment, depression, failure — are crystallized.

As I wrestled with the questions my mail raised and, at the same time — for other reasons — read the mystical literature of the major spiritual traditions, the whole cycle of life learnings that make up the human enterprise became more and more clear. In every culture, the essence of holiness, the ground of maturity, lies not so much in avoiding sin as it does in the cultivation of spiritual consciousness.

I have learned a great deal from the questions posed by my letter-writing readers. I have learned even more from the wisdom figures of past ages and other traditions who, long before all of us, were also trying to find the answers to such things. They, too, struggled to find their way through the vagaries of life led only by the holiness models before them. It is not that they were great sinners who repented; it was that they were great seekers who sought to grow beyond the husk to the core of life, beyond the manuals of the spiritual life to the essence of the spiritual life.

For those who also seek for answers to questions beyond their own "here and now," I offer the concerns of my readers as a template by which to chart the seriousness of our own soul-searchings.

More than that, I offer the responses of those from other times and other traditions as well, who, having sunk into the most radiant shafts of the spiritual light that formed them, extracted its wisdom and grew in its beauty as a sign to the rest of us that we can do the same. Every major spiritual tradition — Hinduism, Buddhism, Judaism, Christianity, and Islam — brings a special gift to the art of living the spiritual life. Each of them refracts the light of its own spiritual wisdom texts in particularly sharp and distinct ways. Each of them strikes a different tone in giving the great truths of life that form a chord, a symphony of truth.

This book will draw from the wisdom literature of each of these traditions in the hope of shedding new light in new ways on life's age-old but continuing universal queries.

It is an enlightening excursion, this wandering into the spiritual insights of other whole cultures, other whole intuitions of the spiritual life. It depends for its fruitfulness on openness of heart and awareness of mind. But the journey is well worth the exertion it takes to see old ideas in new ways because it can bring us to the very height and depth of ourselves. It can even bring fresh hearing, new meaning to the stories that come down to us through our own tradition.

A Sufi story defines the process clearly:

"Tell us what you got from enlightenment," the seeker said. "Did you become divine?"
"No, not divine," the holy one said.
"Did you become a saint?"
"Oh dear, no," the holy one said.
"Then what did you become?" the seeker asked.
And the holy one answered, "I became awake."

It is the task of becoming awake to our God, to our world, to the wisdom that even now lies within us, waiting only to be tapped, that is the real meaning of our questions. It is, more than that, the one great task of life.

May your journey through these questions bring you to a new moment of awareness. May it be an enlightening one. May you find embedded in the wisdom of the past, like all the students of life before you, the answers you yourself are seeking now. May they waken that in you which is deeper than fact, truer than fiction, full of faith. May you come to know that in every human event is a particle of the Divine to which we turn for meaning here, to which we tend for fullness of life hereafter.

Hindu Wisdom

CHAPTER 1

Why Does My Life Feel So Hectic?

When the phone on the office desk rang, I was in the middle of preparing an agenda for the next community meeting. The monastery felt quiet and calm that day — no one in the halls, no one on the public address system, no one at the office door waiting to see me. It was just the kind of day I needed: I could work at the project all day long, give it good thought, then talk to some of the sisters about the background data to be packaged with the presentation. I would get some extra reading done that day for sure.

Then the phone rang again, a double ring this time — the signal that this call could not simply be put on a "call back later" list. Whatever this call was about needed immediate attention. I shook my head a bit and picked up the receiver.

Would I be willing to comment on a recent document, the AP reporter on the other end of the line wanted to know. "No," I said. "I haven't read it." Would I be willing just to say a few words about the subject itself? he asked again. "No," I said. "I don't comment on a thing unless I've studied it carefully." Would I be willing to read it? he went on. "Of course, I'll read it," I said, "but I don't have it now." Could they send it to me and talk to me about it later? he pressed.

I began to calculate the situation: If they sent it today, Thursday, I couldn't get it till Monday. By that time the meeting would be over and I could take the time to read the thing. "I could do that," I said and we ended the conversation.

As I turned back to organize my notes so I could begin to outline the agenda for the meeting, I heard the fax machine in the office across the hall begin to clatter. "Why is that fax machine pounding like that?" I asked the secretary five minutes later. "Because there's a document coming in for you from New York," she answered me. "It's over seventy pages long already and it just keeps printing."

I remember the shock of it. The person to whom I had just spoken on the phone had already transmitted the document to which I had agreed to respond. The document fed into a machine by one secretary 600 miles away in New York City was already being sorted by another secretary in Erie, Pennsylvania. The handwritten note at the end of the document said that the reporter would call back that afternoon to interview me about the material. There went the day, the quiet, the planning, the calm.

That's hectic. That's the kind of immediacy in which the world lives now. That's pressure. That's the commonplace character of your life and mine in this day and age.

I learned a lesson that day that has given grist to my soul for years. There is a difference between the "immediate" and the immediate, between what we mean by instant and what we mean by important. All the old calculations of time upon which we planned our lives, made our schedules, and organized our work dockets have simply fallen victim to the fax machine, the telephone, the email, the automobile, and the airplane. Everything is simply too fast, too near, too accessible now. Time and distance do not protect us from the whirligig called "life" that spins around us now, however far away we may think ourselves from the center of it.

As a result, we have forgotten, if we ever knew, that everything that is possible is not necessary.

"In the early days," I heard a man say, "if you missed the stagecoach, you simply settled down to wait for the next one. After all, there was no problem. They ran every six months. Now," he went on, "people get excited if they miss one section of a revolving door."

The humor is refreshing, of course, but delusory. The insight is not funny. It's a serious one. We have given our souls away to distraction, interruption, rapidity, and clutter. We have become the puppets on our own strings. We have abandoned the calm of reflection for the mirage of the instantaneous.

The truth is that nothing really important in life is done instantaneously. The instantaneous is about satisfaction, not about quality. It caters to our impulses. Whatever urges torment us, we can express. Whatever crosses our mind, we can say. Whatever we want, we can get without stopping to weigh its real value. The instantaneous is about our anger, our emotions, our urges, our instincts, our needs, perhaps, but it is not about diligence. It is not about reflection.

Great life decisions, significant life interactions, require a person to go down into the soul where noise is not a value. There are motives to be assessed there: my own. Why am I even thinking about doing this thing, confronting this person, making this move? What will happen to me if I do? Will I be more of a person — or less — because of it? Will my own life be more soul-centered or not because of it?

And if I decide against it, what then? How do you tell a world rumbling by at high speed, a world that expects action, not thought, that this moment, this situation, demands more than reflexive response? How do you make the point that you need more than the opportunity to talk now, that what you really need is space to think now? How do you slow to a walk a world on a headlong plunge toward chaos? How do you decide between what must be done and what can be done? How do you choose what will really enrich your life in deep-down important ways as well as enrich the lives of those around you in serious and lasting ways?

It's not an easy question. It is easy, of course, to be cavalier about the way you respond to intrusions on your time that are good enough in themselves but are simply not good for everything else you have already agreed to do: "Just tell people you can't do it," critics say. "Just say you won't do it," your advisors say. But they have missed the question, haven't they? They are talking about time, but you are concerned about life. Your life and the way it goes together, and what it means, and what will happen in the future if you say no now.

Deep down, you fear — you know — that if you refuse this request, the world will simply pass you by. Nothing will really change — someone else will be glad to do what you decline to do. The only thing that will really change is that you will be left out of this party, that promotion, the right crowd, the exciting experience.

Then what?

Then it is time to look at life again. What does real life look like to you in your best moments, your quiet moments? What is it that you yourself actually want — down deep — and how much are you willing to give up to get it? What really gives you life? It's time to consider what makes a thing life-giving and the point when even the life-giving becomes death-dealing for you.

Then it is time to define life differently, perhaps. It's the moment to put down what it is we're doing that can be done but does not really need to be done, at least not by us. We need to ask ourselves what it is that we really do not want to do so that everything else we do can be done with more energy, with more quality, with more inner peace.

We also need to ask ourselves if we have gotten to the point in life that the instantaneous has become normative rather than exceptional for us. It's not that we must never ever take on more than we would ordinarily like to do. That depends on the circumstances of the moment. But when we get to the point that overload is a constant, we have a very important spiritual question to consider.

Quiet, regularity, silence are spiritual disciplines as old as the saints of every tradition. "God," the Hebrew scriptures teach us, "is not in the whirlwind."

In the whirlwind of life, in the hurly-burly of things and people and work, we risk the loss of life itself. We risk the loss of focus. Suddenly, we one day realize, we don't know what our lives are actually about anymore, except that they are about too much. We risk the loss of relationships. We get too busy, too scattered, to attend to the truly human intimacies we need if we are to stay in touch with what it means to be human. We risk the loss of balance. We risk the loss of direction. We risk the loss of what Hindu spirituality points to most clearly and what the mystics of all traditions confront us with age after age — total absorption in the Ultimate Mystery of life.

"In this is everything that is," the fourteenth-century Christian mystic,

Julian of Norwich, reminds us, hazelnut in hand. In this tiny seed is the potential, the promise, of the future. Whatever we choose to do now will affect our lives in time to come, either now or tomorrow or years from now. In this moment is everything that is.

Everything that is to be had in life we already have. It is simply learning to see it, to claim it, that will determine the quality of our lives in the future. Will we be busy? Of course we will. Reflection is not about narcissistic leisure; it is about the concentrated activity of being fully human, of giving our gifts in ways that develop us rather than fragment us.

The Indian Johar Rishi tells the story of the genie with which we all deal in our struggle against the hectic, the disordered:

> Once upon a time, a merchant who was vacationing in a small village went to see the village market. At one place he saw a man with a genie and he asked, "What are you selling, my friend?" "My genie," replied the man.
>
> "Well, what does it do?" the merchant asked.
>
> "Everything you want to get done," the vendor said. "It makes the impossible possible."
>
> "Then why do you sell it?" the merchant said.
>
> "Because I have no ambitions left," the vendor said. "It is a wish-fulfilling genie, but it is very exhausting. It cannot stay idle and all the time it needs a new job, a new project, or otherwise it destroys what it creates."
>
> "I have lots of ambitions, lots of jobs to be done," the merchant said. "I'll buy it." When they reached the place where the merchant stayed, the genie said, "Now, Sir, tell me what I can do for you. Your satisfaction is guaranteed, but before enjoying it you must tell me my next job."
>
> "Your first job," the merchant said, "is to build boundary walls and mark my sites."
>
> The genie clapped his hands and said, "All your sites have been enclosed, Sir. Now tell me the next job."
>
> "You really are a wish-fulfilling genie. I am so happy to have you. Your next job is to create buildings on these sites."
>
> The genie clapped again. "It is done, my master. The factories, the

theatre halls, the swimming pool and markets are all crowded with people."

"Fantastic," said the merchant. "Now I want you to make me king of
the world. Build me a palace. Organize a coronation. Invite all the important people. Bring poets and musicians and let the dancers dance
and entertainers entertain."

The genie clapped again and said, "You have been accepted as the
solemn monarch of planet Earth. Your crown is right here. Dress yourself up and enjoy being the most powerful and important person on
planet Earth. But . . . before you leave, please tell me my next job."

The merchant became numb. All his desires were fulfilled. Suddenly
he remembered the merchant's warning: If he could not keep the genie
employed, everything he had achieved so far would be destroyed.

Drops of perspiration started dripping down his forehead. Only
one person could possibly help him.

"Genie," he commanded, "before I become the emperor of the
planet Earth, I would like to get the blessings of my spiritual teacher.
Please take me to the holy one's cave in the Himalayas."

So the genie clapped again and there he was.

"Bless me, holy one, bless me," the businessman said. "I am in great
trouble. I bought a wish-fulfilling genie this morning and all my desires
got fulfilled. But I bought this genie on condition that I have to keep
him engaged or he will destroy what he has created. And now I don't
know what to do with him."

The holy one was sitting naked on a straw mat and greeted the merchant with a radiant smile.

"Don't worry, my son. It is very easy to provide this genie with a
never-ending job. But first relax," said the holy one.

"I cannot relax," the merchant said. "I am agitated, anxious, excited,
terribly disturbed and afraid. Save me."

"Listen carefully, my child," the holy one said. "Ask the genie to bring
the biggest bamboo pole he can get. Then order him to plant it inside the
ground very firm and tight. After the pole is firmly fixed to the ground,
ask the genie to climb it up and down until further orders. This will keep
him busy and you will enjoy your life undisturbed and fearlessly."

"How stupid I am that I could not think of such a simple solution," the merchant gasped.

"When one is obsessed by fear and anxiety one cannot think of such simple solutions," the holy one said. "First you were blinded by your ambitions and you bought the genie. When the genie became too fast in fulfilling your desires you got scared by the speed with which he carried out your orders. Then you got nervous by the imaginary fear of destruction. Go now and feel free." The holy one paused for a moment.

"But before you go," he went on, "know this. I too have a genie. And I, too, have a pole for it."

Then the holy one opened his hands and showed the merchant his prayer beads.

The story has all the earmarks of a fairy tale — except it isn't. This story is about our lives, about what it is to be an adult in a spinning world. Indeed, we all have a genie. The genie is the desire for achievement, the hope for popularity, the thirst for opportunity, and the hunger for excitement. The genie is also a gaping need for success, for adulation, for exhausting irrepressibility. The genie, you see, is inside of us. So the genie "Possibility" can be bought only at great cost. This is a genie that we pay for with our lives.

Most difficult of all, perhaps, is the fact that before it's over, only we ourselves can tame the genie.

We tame our genie by knowing our boundaries and defining them early. I should have said quite clearly, for instance, at the beginning of my telephone conversation with the reporter that I simply could not read and respond to the new document any time before the following week. I had other obligations to attend to with the kind of care and calm that would have made them pleasant rather than painful to meet.

We must begin, as the Hindu holy one shows us, by absorbing ourselves in the things of life that will continue to count when all the tasks and possessions and positions and honors have gone to dust. We must make room in the present for the things of the eternal.

There will always be interruptions in life, of course. There are always those demands that break into our well-planned schedules and require us to stretch ourselves. There are always distinctions to be made between what must certainly be added to our schedules and what can be added but does not really need to be, does not really add much of life to life at all.

Not to be interrupted by some things — our children, our families, our genuine obligations, our responsibilities to ourselves for space and quiet and leisure — would be immoral. Adding other kinds of things to the present schedule may, too often, only destroy both the pleasure and the quality of everything else that must be done.

Then we begin to feel frazzled, put upon, irritated, rattled.

Why does my life feel so hectic? Because, as the Hindu holy one teaches, we have yet to occupy the genie Possibility with the kind of concentration on the fundamental things of life — like just getting up day after day and going on, steadily, calmly, happily — that are far more valuable to the life of the soul than phrenetic action can ever be.

People who are happy and fulfilled are, of course, always busy growing, giving, becoming, being, and doing what it is they are here on earth to be and do. It is not busyness that destroys us. It is simply being perpetually busy with things that only scatter rather than deepen us. This is what makes the difference between doing what we are meant to do and doing everything we can do.

The Hindu holy one tells us clearly to tie our genie to what we are meant to do rather than to everything on the horizon that can be done. Then "hectic" will become holy soon enough.

CHAPTER 2

Why Does the Thought
of Getting Older Bother Me?

Eddie was a 92-year-old mountain of a man. Age, it seemed, had simply passed him by. At 88 he was still golfing every morning and playing cards with "the boys" every afternoon. He was still holding court in the house in which all his children had been born.

So when, after months of wishing back the cancer in him, he finally gave in to it and slept away, they came from the street and from the state-house to pay their respects. As we carried Eddie to the grave, I knew that it was really Eddie who had been carrying all of us over the years.

Eddie had carried the tradition for us. He showed us the best of Po-land — its spiritual strength, its historic pride, its beautiful poetry — its vigilias and Polish hymns and family customs. He taught us all — Irish, Germans, African Americans — that unless we understand and cultivate what each of us had inherited from wherever we came from, we could not really give the world back everything it needed to find in us.

Eddie carried the best of the faith for us. Day in and day out he pursued the spiritual life in the steady, mundane ways we all do. But he did it all the time.

Eddie carried a sense of family for us. He was, in fact, the only man of his generation I ever knew for whom "fatherhood" was his self-definition. He was as clearly and as certainly defined by his fatherhood as a woman had ever been defined by motherhood. Fatherhood was the acme of his life

— not his money, not his job, not his social status, not the size of his house or the prestige of his connections. Just his children really mattered to him: his children, his grandchildren, the children of the neighborhood, and all the rest of us whom he took in, arms open, heart wide.

Eddie carried the culture for us. He was an icon of the intellectual life: he loved opera and reading and art and conversation — especially conversation. And, yes, I know, he was also highly opinionated. But that was because he insisted on being highly informed. He never finished college, but he read more widely than most professors, asked more questions than most scientists, and demanded better answers than most professionals.

He could be persistent, if not downright stubborn about his opinions, yes. He had a way of dismissing every other idea around him that he found not to his liking. "No, no, no, no," he said simply, over and over again. But in the end he always managed to do exactly what he wanted to do: he provoked the rest of us to think a thing through — over and over again.

Finally, Eddie carried for us a vision of what should be, rather than what is. Locally, nationally, globally, his goals were high, his values right.

This man shaped his life around a little corner store on a bombed-out street in the poorest part of town — serving people whom the rest of the country was still refusing drink at water fountains and food at lunch counters. No, Eddie never made a million dollars, but he won a million hearts and changed a lifetime of kids into thinking better of themselves.

When Eddie died, small children and grown men cried.

HELEN IS 92 as I write. She has shrunk in size a bit since I first saw her, fur stole around her shoulders, blonde hair swept back behind her ears, long dark coat swirling as she walked. Helen was the definition of life. No room seemed big enough to hold her.

There was never a lecture she didn't go to, never a speaker she didn't entertain in her own living room, never a question she didn't pursue, never an answer from which she shrank. She seemed hungry for life, as if it were just around the next corner and she simply could not get there fast enough.

The men in her family were all businessmen and Republicans. Helen was a New Deal Democrat. I saw the men venture a skeptical frown at some of the things she said, but I never saw any of them even attempt to argue her down.

Sometime long after most people would have begun to quit living, Helen simply began it all over again. In the late middle years of her life she decided to break the bounds of the small town in which she had lived for almost seventy years. Much as she cared for the place, there was just not enough intellectual air there to sustain a life like hers. So, every summer thereafter she simply moved herself and most of her family to the conference resort center at Lake Chautauqua in New York, where four lectures a day were common fare.

Then she hosted private seminars on her great back porch overlooking the lake. Hardly a scholar or artist has not been touched by her help in one way or another. What she could not do herself, she saw to it that others did.

She thrived on young people and new ideas and unacceptable questions and astonishing answers. She was newness itself.

Except that she wasn't. She was, after all, in her 90s and still prodding everyone in the family, everyone around her, to know more, do more, discover more, be more than they dared to think they were. No dust accumulated on this soul, no entangling fibrils on this mind.

Yet, she told a geriatrician friend who advised her to have a recommending doctor rather than go from specialist to specialist, that when she had gone to a physician they told her to go to a social worker, which she did. And the social worker, at least fifty years her junior, told her that what she needed was to get out more, mix with people and play bingo! "And with macular degeneration!" Helen added.

Helen is not bingo material. She is the idea-agent of the family, the center of intellectual life in her lakeside community, and a philanthropist. Her support launched a Peace Society at a time when patriotism was more a synonym for militarism than for worldwide cooperation. She also started at least two major global projects, the development of which she follows avidly. To tell Helen that what she needs is bingo is akin to telling Henry Ford that what he needs is a go-cart. But it isn't that Helen has no interest in bingo that's sad. What's sad is that younger people would assume, given her age, that she should.

VLADIMIR HOROWITZ, the great expatriate Russian pianist, returned to Moscow in his late 80s to give his first concert there in eighty years. "How did the Russian music critics receive you?" a reporter asked him. "Oh," Horowitz said thoughtfully, "just about the same now as then. When I was five years old they said that I was 'very good for my age.' Now that I am 87 they are saying the same thing." The tendency of the modern world to judge both ends of life as equally incomplete may be the most damning mark of all on our own times.

FROM HELEN AND EDDIE I learned that years are one thing but age is another. It is not years that determine age. Age is an attitude of mind. It is also a repository of sagacity, a mixture of memory and insight.

The Hindus tell a story in the Upanishads that makes the distinction well, I think.

Once upon a time, the people began crying, "There is not enough room. There is not enough room." And it was true. The plants of the plain grew so high and thick and close that no hook or knife was able to clear a path through them. Thick hedges of weed and bramble threatened to choke the trees that towered over them and lock them in an eternal shade of leaves. Food was scarce, for there were few places to grow it.

But that was only a part of the problem. Everything that ever was simply lived and multiplied, growing bigger and bigger, never growing old, threatening to crush the earth itself under the weight of all that teeming life.

The cries of the people grew louder and louder. "There's not enough room. We need more room," they pleaded.

High on her mountaintop, Kali, the goddess of death, sensed the cries of the people and stirred in her sleep. She rushed from her bed and flung open the bedroom window. The sight that met her eyes softened her heart. Piled below her were crowds of people hemmed in by a thick avenue of trees, so tall that they blotted out the sky. Animals of every kind threaded their way warily through the throng. The stench of sweat and the shrill, panicky pleading were everywhere.

Kali turned from the window and called urgently for her servant, Time. "Harness the horses and hitch up the chariot," she said.

Then Kali opened her treasure chest and pulled parcel after parcel from its dark interior until the whole of the room, from floor to ceiling, was piled high with gifts, each gleaming in the gold wrapping that covered it.

When Time brought the chariot to the door, Kali ordered that he fill it with her packages. A single crack of the whip and the horses raced across the face of the sky, carrying them ever downwards to the earth and all its misery.

Kali visited every house, every town, and every village. At each stop she ordered Time from the carriage, his arms full of gifts for all who lived or grew there. Eagerly, the gold wrapping was torn apart to reveal the presents inside. But there was no excited response.

What Kali had brought to the people, what Kali had wrapped as gifts for them, was decay, mold, dust, rust, withered shells, wrinkles, coldness, and aging.

For the first time, leaves changed their color that day and began to fall. The stems of plants grew dry and cracked and turned back downwards to the earth. On that day, too, the people knew for the first time the mark of wrinkles on faces, a stiffness of limbs and joints, and eyes that no longer saw clearly. Soon, too, they discovered death and its pain of loss, at first amongst the animals, and then amongst the people themselves. The elders were leaving, moving aside to make space for the children.

But since then, Kali sends Time ahead of her to warn that Kali is on her way and to present his own special gift, as well, to prepare them for hers. For Time brings the gift of white hair, and he covers it in the golden wrapping of wisdom.

It's a shocking kind of story. What kind of gift is death? What is the purpose of wisdom without eternal life? How would we ever be able to understand one and accept the other or cope with the implications of either?

At first, the story seems obscure, even morose. The people had pleaded desperately for help. But what kind of help was aging and physical deterioration to a people already distressed by the distressing conditions that came with having to deal with timelessness? Until, that is, we begin to understand that there are certain values, clear values, that come only with time, only with age.

Every stage of life is not the same as the one before it. Each of them has its own gifts, its special talents, its particular qualities, which, unless we are willing to age, to pass from one level of existence to another, can never come to fullness. Without them we stay eternal children, our souls do not age and wizen and ripen, our place in society stays static. We remain endlessly alive but endlessly useless to those who come after us.

We mourn youth because we have failed to understand the glory of age.

The problem is clear: we have forgotten how to grow older. We have forgotten how to let go of one stage of life so that other stages can happen — in ourselves and in others, as well. Instead, ours is an age of agelessness, of plastic surgery and health clubs, which, good as they may be for therapeutic reasons, are too often designed to help us fool ourselves into thinking that we will never age, never die. Worse, the benefits of age — white hair and wisdom, the fruit of the various stages of life, the learnings of each separate phase of life we are meant to teach to others — seem to have gotten lost somewhere along the way.

So we try desperately to forget our age, even to deny it. We begin to confuse vigor with agelessness, as if it is impossible to grow older and more beautiful, more valuable, more desirable, more alive as we grow older. Grandmothers dress like teenagers, because they fail to see the iridescence that comes with the beauty of age. Grandfathers join body-building programs, not to stay healthy but to stay young, because they come to confuse physical virility with manliness. Age becomes the enemy. It lurks under every conversation about work, about the future, about value.

Worse, the messages of ageism are everywhere. People over 30 now need not apply for jobs in industries aimed at the youth culture, as if imagination, too, shrivels with the years. Older workers are offered early retirement packages in order to get them out of the workforce, off the payrolls, into intellectual oblivion. Industry makes way constantly for new robots, for electronic gadgetry, for automatic answering programs rather than for the experience age brings to the workplace. And all the while, people can't find human beings to talk to at the other end of the phone anymore and so feel more and more cut off from the whirling changes around them. Even medicine too often confuses the age on the chart with the person in the bed.

"Well, Margaret, I see that someone sent you beautiful flowers," the geriatric physician said to his patient as he made hospital rounds that day. "And well they should to a beautiful woman like you," he added.

"Not exactly, Doctor," Margaret answered. "To tell you the truth, I sent them to myself," she said. "I have noticed that patients who get flowers get more attention from the staff," she went on. "I suppose they figure that people who get flowers are still valuable enough to qualify for care."

We are taught the human uselessness of those over 55, and we learn the lesson well. Experience has been bartered for the glitter of youth. Wisdom has given way to dispensability. Experience comes at great price.

But there is another side of ageism that lurks in this society, affecting our attitudes, curdling even our own appreciation of ourselves. When aging becomes a liability in a corporate culture, youth becomes a low-cost commodity that is forever replaceable. Young workers come cheap to do routine things while machines do the more important ones. Why hire good sense and quick minds, good value systems and well-formed consciences, when we can get young bureaucrats, recruits fresh off the vine, for almost nothing to follow the process and ask no questions?

But the cost of routine is high in a world where imagination and experience and freshness of intuition are the block and tackle of the business world.

There is no place now for reflection on past events in a world devoted only to the immediate, to the eternal "now," to the moment rather than the age.

We learn, indeed, to hide who we really are and what we really have to offer because the world has lost respect for ideas and understanding, for insight and memory.

So we stop in our tracks early. We get old before our time, because, ironically, we fear to get old. So we begin to die in funny little ways long before we begin to die at all. We stop going out. We stop having people in. We stop swimming and fishing and walking and biking for fear we'll be laughed at. "Look at that old lady on a bike!" for example. Or, "Look at that old man running!" for instance. Or, "Look at that old crowd playing shuffleboard!" maybe. Or, on the other hand, "What would she know about long-term investments, in a now generation of thirty-second ads and fast-changing breaking news briefs?"

And yet, it is precisely the question, Why does the thought of getting older bother me? that is the sign that we are ready now for a whole new kind of life. We know that we have begun the move from one stage of life to another. The only thing we fail to realize is that it is up to us to create it. Old age is the age after all-night parties and exhausting job hunting, past the age of child care and professional pursuits, into an age of contemplative leisure and holy wisdom so much prized by the poets and lusted after by the philosophers.

It is the age of coming to understand what kind of person we have become over the years. It is the period in which we stop blaming others for who we are and decide who we want to be now. It is the time for determining what we really believe and why.

Now we can begin to spend our lives on something beside ourselves. Like Helen, we can pursue ideas and enable other people to do that, as well. Like Eddie, we can now spend time replanting the seeds of the past in the present. The new world will not live these values as we did, of course, but we can leave the next generation, if we will, with a vision of what must be carried on if the world is not to swamp itself with the detritus of the superficial.

The Hindu story is clear: we are here to make space for the other, yes. But we are also here to leave them the wisdom one age needs in order to deal with this age. There is great gift in teaching the generation after us not only how to live but also how to die.

White hair and wisdom, wrinkles and stiffness are the signs we show the world that we hold in trust for them the values that count when all the gilding has lost its glitter.

First, of course, we must have the courage to strike out, to refuse to quit prematurely, to develop the wisdom and live the values ourselves. Then death becomes a friend, and the steady but kind decay out of one stage of life into the next one becomes our right to be new and valuable in new and valuable ways again. Then age becomes our final gift to the world.

If the question is, Why does the thought of getting older bother me? the answer must be because I have failed to realize or have lost sight of the strengths gained in the process of a whole lifetime of living well.

CHAPTER 3

What Does It Mean to "Make a Difference"?

I remember the scene well. It taught me a lesson I might otherwise have completely missed.

For a period of time, I drove from Cleveland to Erie on a fairly regular basis, a distance of about 100 miles. Time after time, I put the car on automatic pilot and headed for home, nothing but straight road between me and the priory.

Except for one thing. Every time I made the trip, I began to notice, there was one solitary man standing back off the roadside at the edge of a ragged corn field, a flag in his hand, a sign by his side, one small camp chair open and planted behind him. Trip after trip. Week after week. In cold rain and sleet, in hot sun and wind, there he stood, alone and totally silent. Keeping watch, eloquently silent.

As the weeks went by, I began to slow down as I approached the area. I craned to see what he was selling. Nothing. I tried to read the sign. Weather-worn. I looked for signs of a crowd, an event, something that would give me a clue to what he was about. No one.

One day, I simply turned the car around and went back, drove down the berm slowly, and stopped.

He was not an evangelist, obviously. He was much too quiet for that. He was not a policeman. What he was wearing was definitely not a uniform. He was not a traffic controller. There wasn't a car to be seen for miles. Just one thing stood out: he wore army fatigues, and, on the broomstick standard that he held in one hand while he waved with the other, he flew a home-made flag with a peace sign on it. "Give peace a chance," the sandwich-board sign propped up by the chair read. He himself, I realized as I got closer, had braces on his legs.

He was just one man with one small peace sign standing on an empty road waving a homemade flagpole back and forth at every car that passed.

In my mind, that single man, a veteran I presume, goes on waving ev-ery day of my life. It was his persistence, his dogged refusal to give up waving, his single-minded commitment to changing my mind that got me.

There he stood, in stark contrast to everything else my culture has ever tried to teach me about life: that big is better than small, that strong is more effective than weak, that the ability to make war is more important than the unremitting effort to make peace, that the individual is powerless in the face of juggernauts and corporations and a superpower world.

As a result of having embraced that philosophy of life, we are a nation of grand corporate schemes and huge human fiascos.

We build skyscrapers 100 stories high. Small buildings like the corner store on which so much of our daily lives depend, we never notice.

We count those corporations successful which are international in scope, and everybody else, the local companies and corporations that keep the machinery of local life operating, as wannabes.

Large groups, we figure, are significant. Small groups are nice but, well, frankly, a bit pathetic.

The creation of a vast military machine proves how strong, how right, we are. Talk is weak; negotiation is worse. It's might, size, energy, quantity that counts.

What's big is important. What isn't is hapless. Numbers count. Money counts. One person alone against the world does not count.

No wonder we're all asking the same question: But what can I do — about poverty, about injustice, about peace, about fair labor practices, about equality? I'm powerless. I'm not the one with influence. Nobody lis-tens to me. Nobody thinks the way I do. Nobody cares.

The answer the man on the road taught me, of course, is a simple one.

If we want something to be done we must just do something — one thing, one small thing.

The problem is that so few people really believe that small things have any kind of effectiveness at all. To do small things in a nation of giants seems like the most pathetic sort of all pathetic gestures. To join small groups with global intentions — Greenpeace and its hope to save the environment; Pax Christi and its attempt to call Christians to another, even more Christian, Christian position on war; Amnesty International and its fight against political torture; the Woman's Ordination Conference and its efforts to carve out a voice and place for women in the church — seems almost risible. It carries with it a hint of the insane in an era in which David is a comic figure and Goliath is the norm.

And yet what else is there to do? Except, of course, to do nothing — which is the most potent kind of doing that there is, perhaps, and the most limiting of all, because it dooms us to a motionless present. To do nothing is deadly doing.

The Hindus tell a story of powerlessness that may, in the end, be exactly the kind of spiritual story that created the spiritual Gandhi himself.

Once upon a time, high up in the Himalayas, there lived a tribe of 80,000 monkeys, ruled over by a mighty monkey king. A tree grew in the heart of the valley where they lived by the bank of the river. In the spring, the scent of its white blossoms sweetened the air. The shade of its branches brought a crop of the sweetest and largest fruit in India. The monkeys rejoiced in the good fortune that provided so precious a gift for them.

But the great king warned that if others came to hear of the tree and its fruits, they would want them for themselves and would drive the monkeys away. He feared the men from the cities especially. The monkeys must take care that no fruit ever fell into their hands.

One spring, in the course of culling the tree in preparation for harvesting the fruit, the monkeys missed a flower. By autumn the wizened stem hung heavy with the weight of the fruit on it. Then, suddenly, the fruit fell into the water, and tumbled along on the current to the quiet, wide waters of the plain. There, close to the favorite bathing place of King Brahmadatta, a group of fishermen caught it in their nets.

The fishermen marveled at the size of the fruit, so they brought it to the king. The taste delighted King Brahmadatta, and he decreed that the source of this fruit must be found.

Within days the searchers found the tree. It was still laden with fruit, but a host of monkeys had found it first and, to the horror of the king, were feeding there. It was, he thought, such a waste that those heavenly fruits should feed monkeys. Brahmadatta decided there was only one solution. Next day, they would kill the monkeys so that they would never return to the tree.

The monkeys heard the plot for the next day's slaughter. In great agitation they came to their king and laid it all before him. "We cannot escape," they said. "The distance between our tree and the tree across the stream is too far for us to leap. We shall all die."

For some time the king of the monkeys pondered their plight. Then he made his plan. "I am great-bodied, long and strong," said the king of the monkeys. "Tomorrow those shall all be useful."

At dawn the monkey king made a mighty leap from the fruit tree on this side of the river to a tree that grew opposite on the other bank. On the trunk of the first tree he wound a rope of vine equal in length to his mighty leap. The other end he tied to his ankle.

Again, he gathered his strength and leaped out into space, his long arms reaching for a branch of the fruit tree across the stream. They caught, but as they did, the monkey king realized that the vine rope itself would not be long enough to bridge the gap between the two trees. He had forgotten to allow for the extra length that would be needed to tie the rope to the tree opposite as well as to his ankle.

Now there was only one way to rescue the tribe. Hanging there in space, the king ordered his subjects to run along the vine rope to the bridge of his back and from there, secure in the tree, to save themselves.

For hours he hung there as 80,000 monkeys raced along him until his mighty back could no longer take the strain. As the last of his subjects reached safety, his back failed and the king fell to the ground, limp and broken, in great pain.

King Brahmadatta had watched the escape and the great feat of the monkey king. Now he raced to him. "You have given your life and all your strength to save your people," Brahmadatta said.

"I had to do whatever I could to save them," the monkey said. "My joy is that they are all safe. Now I can rest. You see, Brahmadatta, it is love and not power that makes a great king."

This simple Hindu story defies everything we have ever learned about the indisputability of powerlessness. The fact is that there is always something — some one thing — we can do to make the power of our presence known. Whether it works or not, in the end, it will be the very attempt that makes the difference.

The monkey king had only his own body with which to respond to a force far beyond his own. He had only his own body, one rope, and two trees with which to save 80,000 monkeys from the army of a king. Of course it was impossible. Of course it was foolish. Of course it couldn't be done.

But it was all he had.

The story brings us face-to-face with the heresy of powerlessness that eats away at our sense of self-confidence and, at the same time, justifies our growing unconcern, our refusal to take our portion of responsibility for the human engagements that affect us all.

The question is not, Will what we are doing succeed? The question the story confronts us with is simply, Are we doing everything we can? And will we do it for as long as it takes?

When all is said and done, it is persistence that is the antidote to powerlessness. When I refuse to go on waving, when I pick myself up and leave the field, I have given in. I have surrendered my soul to forces whose only argument is that doing what is wrong is better than doing something else. But it is not the glory of the Chinese government and its use of repression to maintain order that the world remembers — and applauds — after the rout at Tiananmen Square. It is the sight of one young man standing in front of a tank that calls out the monkey king in all of us.

To be the last person on earth opposed to the dropping of a nuclear bomb on innocent people is to preserve more of what it means to be human than can possibly be preserved by using the bomb. It may be the last sign, the most powerful sign, the only regenerating sign the world ever sees, of the valor, the rationality, of which a human being is capable.

In the end, the sight of goodness undeterred has more power than all the forces on earth arrayed against it.

The story of the monkey king who lays down his back so the rest of his world can move from one side of the stream to the other answers the question about personal powerlessness that few ever really want to admit. He was inadequate to the task. He did not have the right equipment. He could not possibly hope to endure. But he tried. And that makes all the difference.

It is only by using what we have in order to do what must be done — whether we succeed or not — that counts. It is putting our own backs into the effort that makes the moral stretch from here to there to anywhere possible.

The truth is that none of us is really powerless. Power resides in the willingness to stand alone until the whole world is forced, just by reason of our unremitting, implacable, stubbornly committed presence, to recognize that there is more to the present question than the answer we have been given and have not explored.

If the question is, What does it mean to "make a difference"? the answer may simply be that I must not allow failure to become more important to me than witness. I feel powerless because the power I do have I do not use. The world needs monkey kings — those who will use whatever little they have to do whatever little they can do — to save the world from the violence that threatens it on every level.

CHAPTER 4

What Does It Mean to
Be a Spiritual Person?

Religion and spirituality are not the same thing. They are, however, commonly confused. "She goes to church every week," we say. "She's a very spiritual person." Or we note that "He's a staunch member of the parish finance committee. He's a very spiritual person." It's an interesting conjunction of unlike ideas. It's the equivalent of saying, "She's an excellent vocalist. She's been taking singing lessons for years." There's certainly a connection between taking voice lessons and becoming a professional vocalist, but it's not a necessary one. The truth is that we can go through the motions about something all our lives and never really become what the thing itself is meant to make us.

Religion and spirituality are like that, too. The one, religion, has to do with leading us to an awareness of God, with giving us the tools, the disciplines to make ourselves ready for the experience of God. The other, spirituality, has to do with transforming the way we live as a result of that awareness, with infusing all of life with a sense of Presence that transcends the immediate and gives it meaning.

Sometimes we stop at one and fail to become the other. We use religious practice as a measure of our spirituality and seek spirituality without the discipline it takes to make it more than some kind of artless escapism. One is as lacking as the other, of course, but religious practice without the spiritual development that is meant to proceed from it is the more deceptive of the two. It leaves us in danger of being keepers of the law rather than seekers of the truth.

It's when we make religion itself our substitute for God that, ironically, our spirits stand to wither or calcify. Ancient Hindu spiritual masters understood the confusion only too well. They wrote:

> Once upon a time, as the Master lay dying, the disciples begged him, for their sakes, not to go.
>
> "But if I do not go," the Master said, "how will you ever see?"
>
> "But what are we not seeing now that we will see when you are gone?" the disciples pressed him.
>
> And the spiritual Master said, "All I ever did was sit on the river bank handing out river water. After I'm gone, I trust you will notice the river."

The story draws a stark distinction between religion and spirituality.

The disciples wanted someone, something to follow. They wanted a law they could live by, a person who could give them orders, a master who would take responsibility for their guidance and their virtue. The master, on the other hand, wanted them to internalize his spirit, not simply to imitate his actions.

The master's meaning is clear: religion is not about following a minister or making a god out of religious practices. Religion is not simply adherence to a code of law that is an end in itself. The Upanishads say: "Unsafe boats are these sacrificial forms." Ritual will not, of itself, take you to the other side.

Religion is meant to be a bridge to God, a vehicle to understanding. It is meant to plumb the depths of the human soul to the source of the spirit. Instead, religion can sometimes even be an obstacle to union with God. As the wag put it, "In order to sin properly it is not necessary to break the rules. All you need to do is to keep them to the letter."

Religion without the spirit it is meant to preserve can become positively irreligious: we put the weak, the wounded, the addicts, the religious others outside the boundaries of our perfect lives, fearful of touching what might pollute us. Religion — who hasn't seen it happen? — can be a very sinful thing.

If religion itself is so necessarily sanctifying, why are there so many wars, so much killing, such unlimited oppression — and all of it in the name of God? Maybe it's because what religion itself loses at times is spirituality — the spirit of the God it preaches. Only when our own hearts are as wide as the God who made us have we become both religious and spiritual.

The difference between religion and spirituality, then, is the difference between neurotic orthodoxy and mysticism. One is religion for its own sake. The other is the immersion of the self into God until we become what we say we are seeking. Real religion is not for the satisfaction of the self. It is for the sake of the world — for, in the Hindu sense, the creation of the kind of personal karma that brings the world to fullness of life.

The orthodox are those who keep the rules and guard the creeds of all the denominations of the world. They know a heretic when they see one.

The mystics of every religion are those who are looking for more than the security that rule-keepers get from being able to go through life keeping count of their virtues. Mystics absorb the spirit to which the rules are meant to lead us. They go beyond theology to immerse themselves in the Reality that the rules are designed to prepare us to see and the theology is meant to describe. They go beyond ritual to the Reality to which it points. They melt into God. They embrace the whole world. They become the love that created the world and the compassion that sustains it. Spirituality is what takes us beyond religious practice to the purpose of religion: the awareness of the sacred in the mundane.

Mystics go beyond the norms of every religion to the God every religion is established to revere. Then denominational boundaries disappear, differences dissolve, theological distinctions become meaningless, and we find ourselves welded to the presence of God here and now — in everything, everywhere, at all times.

Every great religion recognizes the difference between the two. They are all quick to tell one from the other.

The Upanishads, those Hindu scriptures concerned with mystical truth, make the distinction between law and spirit plain. They tell a story about a hermit who worried that, in his study of religion, his son had missed the spirit it is meant to maintain:

Once upon a time, in a hermitage deep in the forest, lived the learned sage, Uddalaka Aruni, with his son Shvetaketu. When Shvetaketu came of age, his father sent him to an Ashram for his education, as was customary in those days. When Shvetaketu returned home after twelve years of education, Uddalaka asked him, "What did you learn while in the Ashram, my son?"

"I learned everything that can be known, Father," Shvetaketu answered.

When he heard this, Uddalaka became silent and thought, "What pride! Such conceit is born only out of ignorance."

"My child, you must get to know the essence of all things, the One that exists in everything in this Universe, the great power of Brahman."

"But Father, if we cannot see the essence, how do we know that it exists?" said Shvetaketu with a puzzled mind.

"I shall explain that to you, my son," affirmed Uddalaka. "First put some water in that pitcher."

"Now bring some salt and put the salt in the water," instructed the father. Shvetaketu did as his father asked.

"Keep the pitcher aside for now," said Uddalaka, "and bring it to me tomorrow morning."

Early the next morning, Shvetaketu went to his father with the pitcher of water.

"Can you see the salt?" asked Uddalaka.

Shvetaketu searched, and, of course, the salt was no longer visible.

Shvetaketu said, "No, Father, it must be dissolved in the water."

"Now taste it from the top," instructed Uddalaka.

Shvetaketu dipped his finger into the water and tasted the water from the top.

"It is salty," Shvetaketu said.

"Now taste the water from the bottom," said Uddalaka.

"It's salty there too, Father," answered Shvetaketu.

"Similarly, Shvetaketu, as you cannot see the salt, you cannot see the essence. But it is always present everywhere."

Finally Uddalaka concluded, "My son, that which you cannot grasp but taste in every drop is the Real. This omnipresent essence is called the Atman, which pervades everything. You, too, are that, O Shvetaketu."

The lesson the story intends to teach is a simple but a profound one. There is something in the universe, the Essence of life, the story tells us, that, living in us, sustains us. It is the subject of religion — but without the spirit of it within us, religion itself is at best wooden, perhaps even useless.

"You too are that," Uddalaka says, and it is suddenly clear. In each of us is the spirit that is the Essence of life. It is more than religious ideas, more than rules, and more than ritual, though each of those things is surely intended to bring us close to it. At base, however, it is only the internalization of the life of the spirit that is the measure of its effectiveness.

Religion is not for its own sake. It is not for the sake of organization or hierarchy, social order or social status. The purpose of religion is to lead us beyond even itself to union with God, to that all-pervading awareness of the spirit of life and truth alive in us now and toward which our lives are directed.

The spiritual person is the person who sees into and under, above and beyond the fixtures and ideas of religion to the sacredness of all of life. The spiritual person is more than a denominational devotee. The spiritual person is one with the universe in all its forms, all its insights. To these people, God is every breath they breathe, every thought they think, every underlying motive of everything they do. They do not seek perfection; they seek the God who is perfect life, perfect fullness, perfect peace.

Spirituality is what takes us beyond religious practice to the purpose of religion: the awareness of the sacred in the mundane, the consciousness of God everywhere, in everyone. It is not the rejection of matter as the opposite of spirit. That kind of spirituality can lead us to devalue the beautiful, the sensual, the physical, and the real. It can even lead us to devalue ourselves. It says that what God has given us to take us to the divine is itself bad. Instead, the spiritual person, as Uddalaka says, is aware of the Essence that pervades everything — including ourselves.

We wonder how it is that religion can do so much violence, feed on so much extremism, lead to such self-destruction. The answer is, of course, that that kind of religion is not about coming to the spirit of God. When religion requires that our humanity with all its joy and all its sense of goodness be stamped out, there is something wrong with that religion. "We are not human beings trying to be spiritual," Jacquelyn Small says. "We are spiritual beings trying to be human."

The spiritual person knows that there is no difference between the sacred and the secular, the material and the spiritual. They are all simply part of the Essence, simply stepping stones along the way to the God who is everything there is or needs to be.

Religion itself is not sacred. And if or when it pretends to be, it can stop a soul in mid-flight from ever being able to find God in the midst of life. Then we make the means the end. Then we take a spiritual process designed to help us find God in life and turn it into God. And that is a weak and pathetic substitute for the very meaning of life, the Essence of all things, the magnate to which our souls cling.

If the question is, What is a spiritual person? the answer is that the spiritual person is the one who breathes in and out the spirit of the God toward which they move.

CHAPTER 5

How Can I Learn to
Let Go of the Past?

Emily, an attractive woman in a black box jacket, silver roll-up collar, black pumps, and a hemline just touching the top of the knee, sat hunched over on the couch, her shoulders sagging, her eyes sad. "Lovely," I thought. "A middle-aged woman who has all the style and twice the class any 25-year-old can possibly muster. In the end," I went on musing for my own satisfaction, "experience and style always trump youth and style."

But, in this case, I found out to my profound surprise, it didn't. This was a woman who, despite all the class with which she carried herself — whatever the poise she had cultivated — lived inside a crushed soul, the pain of which lay there lodged in her eyes for all the world to see.

The situation was a common one. One night the steady, eternally predictable father of her three young children simply walked in and announced he was leaving her to marry another woman. The shock of something like that, of course, can leave a person numb, breathless, unable to think. No wonder she needed support, someone to walk through these days with her, someone who could help her dredge up from the depths of her lifeless heart the thoughts she needed to express, the plans she needed to make. The only trouble, I learned later in the conversation, is that the man had not left her yesterday, or last week, or on her birthday, or six months ago. The man had left her ten years before our meeting. The children who had been ages 8, 10, and 12 then were now young adults, college graduates, professional women themselves.

For ten years, this competent woman and her three children had lived in depression and anger, in desolation and a sense of deprivation, with loss as their only constant companion. Every phone call that never came, every custodial visit that never healed the rift, every birthday present that failed the test of personal care, every holiday that went unnoted, every continuing trace of the inability to separate only made the woundedness deeper, more bitter, worse. The ghost of life past followed them down the winding years like the specter of death.

There was simply no moving on to new plans and happy new beginnings. Life went on, but death had taken over. And now the children were all leaving, too.

After weeks of work with her, I remember feeling immobilized by it myself. Here was someone who had everything — good looks, a good job, good friends, good health, good children — but her soul was cemented in the past. Why? And what could possibly be done about it? Was this love without bounds or life without hope? What do we do when we simply cannot move on in life and, at the same time, simply cannot escape the pain that comes with not moving on?

ANNIE, ON THE OTHER HAND, was another case entirely. Annie had lived alone for a long time now. This husband had left years ago, too. The children were gone, the house had to be given up, the finances had never really kept up with the cost of living. But Annie smiled and smiled. She cultivated women friends, took the bus to the casinos on Wednesdays, played bridge on Thursdays, and worked at church events on weekends.

To many people, it had all the hallmarks of a very lonely life. Finally, Annie's big chance came years later when the widower down the street took a fancy to her. Suddenly, there were fewer nights left for card playing with the "girls" because, it seemed, she was going to one show, one dinner after another, with a man who also liked to smile a lot. It all looked very, very settled. The word was out: there would be a small wedding — just his family and hers, both of which had heaved a sigh of relief that neither of them would be alone anymore — and she would move into his big house.

Then one day I ran into Annie going into chapel. "When's the big day, Annie?" I asked. "Ah," she said. "I've changed my mind. I'm not getting married again. I like the going out but I can do that without doing the socks, too."

TWO STORIES, both real. How do we account for the difference between them? When our own time comes — when change falls unexpectedly, heavily upon us — how do we spare ourselves the grief of one in order to deal well with what are nevertheless the obvious diminishments of the other? How do we recover from the losses life brings along the way?

Hindu spirituality comes to terms with providence quite directly and embeds the process of change into one of the most precious stories of the tradition. The story of Ganesha, the elephant-headed god of India, the divine remover of obstacles, provides a model of acceptance that may explain the calm flexibility that seems built right into the very culture of India. It could, at the same time, perhaps, reduce some of the anxiety of our own. It is a study in making-do, in allowing new things to take the place of old ones.

Shiva, the mighty God of both Destruction and Joy, lived high up in the Himalaya mountains with his beautiful wife, Parvati. Sometimes, life was not much fun for her. Shiva was often away for years at a time on his usual business of creating and destroying people or dancing on top of the world to keep it going.

On one occasion Parvati did not know when he might return. She was bored. There was not much she could do all by herself on a mountain peak. On this particular day, she was feeling unusually lonely.

Finally, the perfect solution dawned on her. "I will make myself a baby," she cried with happiness. "I will make myself a baby boy."

Parvati found some clay and water. She pounded the clay until it was soft and pliable and then she began to shape a baby. The first form she made looked too ordinary and not cuddly enough. So she began to add clay to its stomach until it was fat and round. Parvati laughed to herself. She was beginning to love the baby already.

She put the baby in the sun to dry. Soon it opened its eyes and began to smile. Parvati was overjoyed. She had found the perfect playmate. She cooed to it, talked to it, and spent many hours laughing at its antics. Several years passed this way.

One day, Parvati took her son for a long walk. When they came to a pool of water Parvati, hot and tired, wanted to stop and bathe in it, so she placed her young son on guard. "Don't let anyone come near the pool while I am bathing," she said, so the roly-poly boy sat down upon a large flat stone while his mother made her way into the refreshing water.

Just then it happened that Shiva was finally returning home. He heard splashing and was about to walk towards the water when he found himself stopped by a fat little boy. "Don't go any further," the boy ordered.

Shiva was not accustomed to taking orders. He tried to brush the boy aside but the boy resisted and fought back. Shiva's anger began to mount. Suddenly, without warning, Shiva drew out a sword and cut off the boy's head.

Parvati, hearing a commotion, slipped into her clothes and rushed towards the boy. She let out a scream and fell sobbing to the ground.

Shiva realized that he had done something terrible but did not know what it was. What could he possibly have done to upset her so?

"You have murdered our child." Parvati was quite hysterical by now. "Our child?" Shiva bellowed. "You say that I have killed our child. But we have no child!"

"Of course we have," Parvati said. "We have a child because I made one. I made one because I was lonely. I was lonely because you were away."

Parvati was disconsolate, and Shiva was distraught. What could possibly be done about it now? Then Parvati said to Shiva, "Go out into the forest with your mighty sword. I want you to cut off the head of the first living creature you see and bring it back. Fit the head onto our child and give it life. That is what I want. If you do not do this for me, I will never speak to you again."

Shiva went racing into the forest with his mighty sword looking for a living creature. But, tragedy of tragedy, the first living creature he saw was an elephant. He could do only what was doable. He cut off the elephant's head and, dutifully, brought it home. There he fitted the head onto the child's body, breathing life into it as he did so, and waited for his wife's reaction.

To his surprise, Parvati began to stroke the child's trunk and the child began to laugh. This boy, Parvati discovered, was, in some ways, even better than her first creation.

Shiva sighed with relief. By this time, he was beginning to get very fond of the child himself.

The story sounds very foreign to the Western mind at first. But, if truth were known, the story is so often our own. We, too, create for ourselves what we think we need to make the perfect life. We shape it and form it. We pursue it and persist at it. We fence ourselves around with what we believe are the only things that can ever really make us happy. And we cling to them.

What we forget is that nothing is forever. Everything is for its own time only. Life is made of many stages — which is why life does not end when the stage and places of our shaping disappear into the mist of an ongoing life shaped by other people and other circumstances beyond our own.

Every emotionally healthy individual someday, somehow finds herself faced with accepting an elephant child — or no child at all. We all lose things — great things — along the way. Parents die, houses burn down, companies close, relationships end. Then we find ourselves with lives cobbled together out of strange materials that bring back what we had before but in entirely new ways. We meet an old woman who begins to care for us like one of her own, perhaps. We move to new towns and find even better places to live, maybe. We go back to school to learn new skills and get ourselves a far more interesting job. We meet someone new.

The process is called "life."

I have a friend who defines Divine Providence as whatever happens once we have tried with all our might to prevent it. The definition is a revealing one. There are simply some things in life that cannot be avoided. Death happens. Sickness happens. Loss happens. Change happens. Then, it is not a matter of being able to control life that we need; it is a matter of being able to accept what can be made out of what's left of it.

Parvati had made a perfect world for herself. She had created what she wanted, whatever its effect on anyone else around her. When part of the world she loved, the child, was destroyed by the other part of the world that she had also loved, her husband Shiva, the pain of it was almost more than she could bear. Only because Parvati was willing to allow one joy to be substituted for another could a new future emerge out of tragedy. No, it wasn't the same future; it was a different one from what either Parvati or Shiva had planned. But it was, in its own way, just as good, if not better.

When we refuse to let go of the past, when we refuse to build a new life in the place of the old, we doom ourselves to the kind of emotional death from which there is no exit. We entomb ourselves. We make new life, new spirit, new spiritual insights impossible. We fail to see the God of the present as the new gift of the past.

Emily refused psychologically to leave a marriage long dead. As a result, she lost years of her life embalmed by the loss of it. No elephant child for her. Annie, on the other hand, moved on to a new life and, in the end, discovered that it was a truer life for her than trying to recapture what had been but could never be again.

Why is it so hard for me to let go of the past? Because I cling to it long after it's gone. I fail to realize that there is really no such thing as the past; there is only the present out of which to make a life. It's hard for me to let go of the past because, despite the fact that every step of life has been right for me in the past, I refuse to trust that the next one will be right, as well. I seem to think that I have always been in control of my life, when, as a matter of fact, every major part of life — my birth, my upbringing, my relationships, even my present circumstances — have all been happenstance and I have survived — thrived — on them all.

How can I learn to let go of it? Easy, Hindu spirituality tells me. All I need to do is to embrace the future with the knowledge faith gives us of the rightness of the past. Why? Because God is waiting for me here and now, in this new place, in this new moment, just as God has always been there in the past — to give me new insights, to give me new joy.

If the question is, How can I learn to let go of the past? the answer is simply that I must surrender the future to the God who created the past I so love and who will companion me yet into the future I fear.

Buddhist Enlightenment

CHAPTER 6

Would I Do It All Again?

"If I had it to do over again," the doctor told me in the lobby of the city's largest hospital, "I would not be going into medicine." This man was one of the most respected physicians in the city, a neurologist and brain surgeon whose history of life-and-death cases touched everyone in town, if not directly then indirectly, at least. His house on the hill had a winding driveway up to the front door and a horse paddock in the back field. This was not a man you would expect to hear question whether he should have done his life differently. He was, to all intents and purposes, stable and successful, fully in charge of his very rewarding life.

Andy, on the other hand, was just like the doctor — only different.

"Andy?" the mother said. "Oh, I never know what Andy is going to do next. He started out in accounting but he never really liked it. So then he did sales." She paused. "Now he's talking about taking up art." Andy, well into his 30s by now, had moved back into the family home. One wife had already disappeared. He saw their two children regularly but not enough to really think of himself as their father. A new girlfriend stood listlessly by, merging into the relationship, but with very little energy. Two rudderless boats in a storm, it seemed. "I know it's bothering him," the mother finished, but I could tell by the way her voice dropped when she said it that, most of all, it was bothering her. How was it that a young man of his background, of her care, was floundering so badly?

Ellen fit the pattern of try and fail, start and stop, search and doubt, too. No wonder she came to the reunion with no small amount of hesitancy. She had left the convent years ago. To be invited back to join the community for the order's anniversary touched two nerves: What would they think of her now? Had she failed both herself and them by her infidelity? The girl she entered with, her best friend then, had stayed, was still there, would be at the party. How would she feel when she saw her after all these years? She had loved the sisters, but the life, good as it was, never really seemed to fit for her. Or was it she who had not made herself fit? Had she made a terrible mistake by leaving it?

I know those feelings. In most monasteries, as in most marriages, we celebrate our silver and golden anniversaries of final profession. I remember explaining to a congregation at one of those celebrations that the only difference between the two is that after twenty-five years a person says to herself, "Well, it hasn't been too bad so far. I might as well go on with it." And that after fifty years, she says, "I've thought it over and I've decided to stay." Everybody laughed because everybody there, if the world only knew it, had gone through the same kind of thinking themselves sometime in life. The fact is that someplace along the line we all live life backward. We look back and we wonder.

When we're young, everything is about the future. It's where we're going next that counts. In early middle age, the big question in life is whether we are where we're supposed to be. In later years, the question is, What did we miss, what could we have done other than what we did? Then, after years in a marriage or a career or a place, the question is almost inevitable, Why didn't I do all the other things I could have done?

We start to wonder what would have been, what could have been. We wonder if what we did was really the right thing for us to do, the wrong thing to do, the only thing to do, the good thing to do. We play with different scenarios: Where would I be now if I had married the other one, gone to a different school, taken a different job, moved to a different place?

And all the play-acting comes out to the same place. To here. To now. What else? Of course. But is that certainty or simply resignation? Most of all, does it matter now what it is?

It's an interesting game, this slipping in and out of all the other worlds I might have lived in, but didn't. More than that, though, I think the exercise of trying on one life after another, at least in my mind, may be an important one as well. It may, if we're honest with ourselves, be the only thing that can possibly save us from wishing our lives away rather than living them to the hilt.

The Buddhists tell a story that gives meaning to the process, I think:

The master of Kennin temple, Mokurai, had a protegé by the name of Toyo. Toyo was very young when he came to the temple. But seeing the older disciples visit the master's room each morning and evening to receive instruction in Zen or to ask for personal guidance, he wanted to do the same. All of the disciples were given koans to help stop their minds from wandering to useless things. Toyo was eager and wanted to do zazen, as well.

"Wait a while, till you're older," the master said. "You are too young for such problems."

But the boy insisted, so the teacher finally gave in.

Every evening, then, Toyo went at the proper time to the door of Mokurai's room. He struck the gong to announce his presence, bowed respectfully three times outside the door, and then went to sit before the master in respectful silence.

"You can hear the sound of two hands when they clap together," said Mokurai. "Now show me the sound of one hand."

Toyo bowed and went to his room to consider the problem. From his window he could hear the music of the geishas. "Ah, I think I have it!" he told himself.

The next evening, when his teacher asked him to illustrate the sound of one hand, Toyo began to play the music of the geishas.

"No, no," said Mokurai. "That will never do. That is not the sound of one hand. You've not got it at all."

Thinking that such music might be interrupting his thought, Toyo moved his abode to a quiet place. He meditated again. "What can the sound of one hand be?" he thought. Then he heard some water dripping. "I have it," imagined Toyo. "That must be it."

When he next appeared before his teacher, Toyo imitated dripping water.

"What is that?" Mokurai said this time. "That is nothing but the sound of dripping water. That is not the sound of one hand. Try again."

In vain Toyo meditated to hear the sound of one hand. He heard the sighing of the wind. But the sound was rejected.

He heard the cry of an owl. This was also refused.

The sound of one hand was not the locusts either.

Week after week after week, Toyo visited Mokurai with different sounds. All were wrong. For years he pondered what the sound of one hand might be.

At last Toyo explained to Mokurai, "I can collect no more sounds. I have reached nothing but soundless sound."

"Ah," said the master, "finally you have reached true meditation."

Suddenly Toyo realized that he had finally heard the sound of one hand.

It's a subtle little story but an impacting one, nevertheless. Toyo sets about doing something when he is actually far too young to completely understand what it is he is trying to do — or why, or how, or for what purpose.

Only when there is nothing else he has to learn there, only when he has given the enterprise everything he had to give, did he really become what he wanted to be: a meditator.

The task of life, whether Toyo realized it or not, was simply to get the most out of what was at the moment. It was not to wrench it to be something it was not.

The Buddhist master knew what we have yet to understand when we ask ourselves, looking back over life, if we would really do the same thing again. The real answer is that what we really need to understand is that it wouldn't make much difference whether we did or not. Whatever we did, we would be the same person doing it. Wherever we went, we would still have the same things to learn that we have learned here and now in the situation we're in. And finally, we would still take the same amount of time to learn our particular life lessons as we have in this situation, because the lessons are the lessons and we are who we are, wherever we go.

Like Toyo, we all start young — so eager, so sure of ourselves. Life, we think, is simply a series of tasks to perform, a list of things to do: get the job, buy the house, finish the degree, have the children, do the work. It takes years to figure out, if we ever do, that life is not a task at all. Life is far more difficult than that. Life is the process of coming to see what is not seeable, to hear what is not said, to become what we are but never knew we were.

Instead, we go through life collecting all the things we imagine it must be about. Some of us seek sounds of success; some of us want sounds of coins rattling in our pockets; some of us hear sounds of flattery; some of us expect it to be sounds of power. But none of those sounds tells us much about life at all, about what it is to be able to walk through life without harming ourselves or anyone else in the process.

When we look back, not uncommonly, we see that we have failed at one thing after another. We are tempted, like Toyo, to think that failure is what it has all been about. The marriage had a rocky part. The vows ceased to matter for a while. The children rebelled, embarrassed us, cast aspersions on our parenting. The family rejected us. The social prestige never really came — or at least never stayed long enough to become firm and unassailable. What had once been unquestionable — the love, the work, the institution — became along the way more a commitment of convenience than conviction. We stayed where we were because there was nowhere else to go — either because it was too soon or too late, too risky or too dull, too expensive or too mundane.

So, like Toyo, we stayed. We got older. We got quieter inside. We got mellow. We came to terms with all the losses, all the questions, all the dulled ambitions, all the second-rate achievements, all the public invisibility, all the little secrets of our lives.

Then, one day, we gave up reaching for the unreachable. We left off grasping for snowflakes. We quit struggling to hold on to what was not ours to own. We quit crying about what we didn't do, what we didn't know, what we never got. Then we began to understand that life is more than its failures, more than its trophies.

Life, it became clear, has something to do with accepting its impermanence, learning to move on in both mind and body, accepting who we are and forgiving ourselves for who we are not. Then, we began to be happy.

Impermanence, the Buddha teaches, is the great lesson of life. Nothing comes and stays forever. It doesn't matter how much power we get. It will go as it came, quietly and undeserved. We won't notice anymore how much money we have. There is only so much money a person can spend and only so much spending that can get us what we need rather than what we want. We will lose, eventually, however much influence we have managed to garner. It will dissolve before our eyes as one generation replaces another. Our "connections" will lose their influence as well. Life — right now, this moment — is sifting through our fingers like sand in an hourglass.

It is not simply having life that determines the quality of our lives. It is learning to let it go, one phase at a time, that determines the measure of our contentment, the value of our insights, the caliber of our faith. Learning to be more than what we have or do is the real beginning of life.

In Buddhist terminology, life is the process of becoming awake to what is really real, to what is good, to the foolishness of calling anything final or permanent or necessary or imperative. "It is what it is," the Buddha says.

Everything is for now, nothing is forever. Learning to live in the now, seizing it, realizing its value, honoring its presence in our lives makes for fullness of life.

In the West, the present moment is meant only for the achievement of a future moment. So we are forever looking forward with fear of failure or looking back with regret for our failures. But what is failure, really, but the judgment that what has happened was wrong for us when, in fact, it may have been the most right thing of all?

The things that made me what I am, that brought me to the silencing of my ambitions, the quieting of my restlessness, the damping of my desperate attempts to have more and more and more, would have happened anywhere, true. If not here, somewhere else would have been just the same, demanded just the same from me, freed me from myself — if I would allow it — just the same.

But these things didn't happen elsewhere. They happened here. After all, it's not where I am that is in question. It's about whether or not I have finally come to realize what life is really about — no matter where I am.

If the question is, Would I do it all again? the answer must certainly be, well, why not?

CHAPTER 7

How Do I Know the Right Thing to Do?

Most of the mail I get is from people who are disturbed about the state of the country or confused about the position of the church on major social issues. And they all want to right it. Some of them want to do it by changing the institutions as we have known them. Others simply want to leave them. Some of them want the old world back. Many of them want a new one entirely.

Whatever their political or theological positions, however, most of them feel powerless to do anything or, worse, unsure what's really right to do, even if they felt they could change things. All of them are trying to figure out what they can do to resolve the issues, to live with the situation in peace themselves. They don't write out of anger. They write because most of them feel uncertain about their own responses to the world around them, as well as concerned about what they see happening.

One woman wrote, for instance: "I am at a point in my life where I am deciding if I want to continue to be an active Catholic. I am not connecting spiritually and I have no spiritual community. I do not go to mass anymore though up until two years ago I went weekly."

Her story is not a new one. It's of every ilk and stripe, every denomination and nationality, every political body and social movement. Everywhere people are trying to reconcile the worldview with which they grew up with a worldview in flux.

Things are not the same anymore: a country once the idol, the model, the savior of the world has become a country on the defensive everywhere. People who once admired — and still envy, or at least resent — the wealth and success of the United States are now asking whether the country got them honorably or at the expense of the rest of the world.

All of Christianity itself, not simply a few troubled denominations, is under a new kind of scrutiny, if people are bothering to pay much attention to the church at all. It is Christian countries that developed the atomic bomb — at least as much for experimental purposes as for political reasons — and have threatened to use it again. It is Christian countries that have filled their coffers with the resources of developing countries and then charged the same countries exorbitant prices for the products made from those raw materials.

It is the Christian world that is developing genetically modified seeds. The rest of the world — Hindu, Buddhist, Jewish, Islamic — knows that genetically modified seeds are capable of feeding the entire world. But they also know that they are capable of starving the entire world, as well, once organic seeds are destroyed and genetically modified seeds are patented by Western companies. Then, since genetically modified seeds are not naturally produced and so cannot reproduce themselves, the West will have a monopoly on all the food in the world as well as all the money and all the technology and all the products and all the power.

It is Christian churches, often, as much as any other, that equate the flag and the cross, that subordinate women in both home and church, that seek to impose a kind of Christian theocratic state in a pluralistic world.

Indeed, what is right and what is not has become the problem of the twenty-first century. What to do about it has become the problem of the individual seeker.

The woman's letter went on: "On Christmas Day I attended church with my mother, who is a devout churchgoer, and my sister and her family and my own family. It was nice to be back in the familiar congregation until the new minister got up to give the sermon. His sermon was an absolute disgrace. He should be reprimanded. However, there is little hope of that. I would have gladly stood up and walked out during it but I did not want to upset my mother and daughter. After church I found out my mother was so upset she would have joined me and so would all of my family and some neighbors. . . . I should have done the right thing and walked out."

The implications of the letter were clear: we should be doing the right things.

But how do we know what is really the right thing to do in difficult situations? What do we do when the path is not clear, when there are two answers to everything — each of them equally intense, each of them equally defensible, each of them equally sincere?

At one time, as some people remember, there was just one thing to do and we all knew what it was: obey. But there is not just one answer to much of anything anymore. There are values in conflict now. Shall we have order — meaning obedience — or justice? Equality or complementarity? The priesthood of believers or clericalism? Evolution or Intelligent Design? Higher wages or greater profit taking? Research or development? Our way or theirs?

When we are faced with choosing between one answer that accepts the reality of what is and another answer that is committed to the vision of what should be, then what? Do we accept the given order because it is the given order or do we press for change? What's right? And how can I know it?

The Buddhist masters tell a story that reflects both the depth and the eternal value of the question:

Shoun became a teacher of Soto Zen. When he was still a student his father passed away, leaving him to care for his old mother. Whenever Shoun went to a meditation hall after that, he always took his mother with him. She could not be left alone, so she accompanied him on his journeys. When he visited monasteries, therefore, he could not live with the monks.

So he would build a little house and care for her there. He would copy sutras, Buddhist verses, and in this manner receive a few coins for food.

When Shoun bought fish for his mother, the people would scoff at him, for a monk is not supposed to eat fish. But Shoun did not mind. His mother, however, was hurt to see others laugh at her son. Finally she told Shoun: "I think I will become a nun. I can be a vegetarian, too." So she did and they studied together.

Shoun was fond of music and was a master of the harp, which his mother also played. On full-moon nights, they used to play together.

One night a young lady passed by their house and heard music. Deeply touched, she invited Shoun to visit her the next evening and play. He accepted the invitation. A few days later he met the young lady on the street and thanked her for her hospitality. Others laughed at him then, too. He had visited the house of a woman of the streets.

One day Shoun left for a distant temple to deliver a lecture. A few months afterwards he returned home to find his mother dead. Because his friends had not known where to reach him, the funeral service was already in progress.

Shoun walked up and hit the coffin with his staff. "Mother, your son has returned," he said.

"I am glad to see you have returned, son," he answered for his mother.

"Yes, I'm glad, too," Shoun responded. Then he announced to the people about him: "The funeral ceremony is over. You may bury the body."

When Shoun was old he knew his end was approaching. He asked his disciples to gather around him in the morning, telling them he was going to pass on at noon. Burning incense before the picture of his mother, he wrote a poem:

> For fifty-six years I lived as best I could,
> Making my way in this world.
> Now the rain has ended, the clouds are clearing,
> The blue sky has a full moon.

His disciples gathered about him, reciting a sutra, and Shoun passed on.

Shoun may be a contemporary model of what it means to live a holy life in a changing world. Here was a man recognized to be holy who never really did anything "right."

Every law of life to which he had committed himself he broke in favor of an even greater law: love for his mother, responsibility to others, kindness and compassion for the wounded and marginalized.

He was a vegetarian who ate fish because fish was good for his elderly mother, who, with the death of his father, was now in his care.

He was a monk who did not live in the monastery because he could not leave his mother alone.

He was a celibate who, totally contrary to monastic law, went to the home of a prostitute to play the music she loved because her soul was more important than her body to him.

Then, having missed his own mother's death because of his teaching responsibilities, contrary to Buddhist custom he abandoned all the traditional funeral rituals in favor of the more simple way of living the faith that had been the hallmark of both her life and his.

Shoun lived all his life simply doing what he had to do as well as he could do it. He did not posture; he did not pretend. He lived Buddhist values but not necessarily Buddhist practices. What he was as a Buddhist marked him, not what he did that was Buddhist. He did not practice compassion; he lived it. He did not talk about mindfulness; he became it.

Was he perfect? No. The Buddha, in fact, did not really believe there was such a thing as perfection, if by perfection we mean meeting the expectations of others. The real enlightenment, the Buddhist believes, is coming to understand that we cannot be anything other than what we are. We are all that we have, but what we are is the stuff of which the fullness of life is made.

What we are, such a spirituality implies, is more than enough as long as we realize that the real achievement of life does not lie in practices and asceticisms and rituals, in trying to fit someone else's pattern or thoughts or goals. It lies in realization of the impermanence of life and in refusing to cling to anything — good as it may have been at one time. It lies in embracing the demands of every moment as one thing becomes another, rather than trying to freeze life at any moment of time. It lies in being able to find holiness in the mundane: eating the fish, respecting the prostitutes, even breaking the little rules so that the greater demands of life can be honored. Shoun says it best: "For fifty-six years I lived as best I could."

What is right is only that which must be done at the present moment, even when we are not sure exactly what that is. It is about living the best we can in circumstances that demand more than what we have at the ready.

Clearly my letter-writer friend had already arrived at a kind of rightness she never really dreamed of having. She wrote in her final paragraph: "I decided to take action and support the abused. I don't want to wait anymore — I want to find a place where my family and I can go weekly to connect with a community and discuss religious issues and connect spiritually. . . . I do not see a place for this in my parish."

How can anything that stretches the self and does not destroy the other be anything but "right" — at least for now? When the circumstances change, as they inevitably will, integrity may well demand another answer. If the question is, How do I know the right thing to do? the answer must be, at least until the present circumstances change, that we must, with Shoun, do the best we can.

CHAPTER 8

How Do I Know Who to Follow?

I have become accustomed to people asking for clarification of ideas or recommendations for bibliographies. This question was of a different sort entirely. The letter was short and to the point. The writer wanted me to recommend a church, a pastor, a liturgical style, a theological climate, a place where her soul would grow.

The letter said simply: "I have heard you speak several times on Wisconsin Public Radio. . . . I'm a born [Christian] but have many doubts regarding my church. I no longer 'feel' right there. Could you direct me to some other churches in [this] area? I have searched but find it very difficult. People are reserved when speaking openly."

End of letter maybe, but the beginning of a much larger question: Can anyone really recommend a spiritual life for anyone else? Should they even try?

Maybe it is the search itself that is the spiritual medicine we need. Maybe the spiritual style we find but do not like is really what we need if we are ever to become thinking Christians ourselves. Maybe the sense of aloneness with God is actually more important than going to church at all at some periods in our lives. Maybe what we need more than the map to any particular parish or minister is to find someone who will help us understand what it is in each place we go that either attracts or repels us, that shows us the face of God or does not.

When the spiritual life becomes ideological rather than personal, is it really a spiritual life at all? When we're all busy selling our brand of religion — rosary beads or no rosary beads, statues or no statues, square churches or round churches, art or no art — what is left, then, for seekers to find for themselves? And if we do not find our own way of touching God, do we really have a personal spiritual life at all?

What is left for God to do in the soul when someone who stands between us and God has already decided how and where God will really be with us in life?

The temptation, of course, is always to let someone else determine the nature of our spiritual life. After all, it feels so much safer to turn our conscience over to someone else rather than to take responsibility for forming it ourselves. "What if we're told to do something we believe is wrong?" I asked our novice mistress years ago. "Then the one who gives you the command will be accountable for it. Your obligation is simply to obey." But that answer is far too easy. If all I have to do is to listen to someone else, then what happens to the anguish of decision? What happens to witness? What happens to the purpose for which we have been born? For what are we really responsible? Or is free will only a sham?

Yet, at the same time, who can afford to be a law unto themselves? We cannot form a conscience out of nothing. There is the wisdom of the past to consider. What decent human beings have found to be important throughout time is no small restraint on human endeavor and personal license in the here and now. But even then, it is not simply what the human community before us has done that makes it right. Maybe, at that moment in time, under those conditions, it was right only for them — like the patriarchs of the Hebrew Testament, Abraham, Isaac, and Jacob, and their many wives, for instance.

It is why groups did a thing and what they knew when they did it that determines its present value. For generations, for instance, in every people, pre-scientific culture defined women as lesser human beings, blacks as partial persons, children as simply small adults. With that kind of thinking, the ownership of blacks, the control of women, and child labor systems are all moral or, if not moral, at least understandable. In some parts of the world, those positions still prevail — but this time not without contention. Now there is information that simply undermines, negates, the moral foundation of such behavior. Children are developing persons, not fully developed adults. Blacks are not inferior human beings. There is no genetic difference between the races. They have the same potential, feelings, intelligence, and human nature as every other person on earth. They cannot be owned or used as slaves. Women are not "misbegotten males," as Thomas Aquinas argued on insufficient scientific data. They are as fully rational and totally equivalent human beings as males and must be treated as such in all instances. To do anything other than that is, indeed, to be immoral.

These types of questions arise in every generation. We no longer ask if a black person or a yellow person or a red person is fully human. But we ask questions very much like it. Is a fetus a person or not? we ask our own generation. Is stem cell research ethical or irresponsible? When is sexual behavior debased and when is it not? Is the use of a condom moral or immoral? Is capital punishment really a deterrent to crime, and even if it were, can it possibly be moral? Do animals have rights?

The truth is that every age lives with questions in progress.

Some of those questions will eventually be decided by science. The problem is that we don't know when. So we must all form our decisions on the best data available: the wisdom of the ages, the present findings of science, the highest ideals of our hearts, the best moral guides we have. But in the end, before the bar of humanity, each of us will be responsible for our own decisions.

In a sense, then, conscience — morality — is the easiest spiritual question of them all. But the problem is that there are two kinds of spiritual questions. One has to do with right and wrong, with keeping the rules, with living an ethical life. The other, more difficult question, however, is how to become a spiritual person. How do we become the kind of people who, by breathing in harmony with God, by breathing in tune with the universe, by being aware of God in every breath we take, come to the point where we breathe out goodness? Then, we ourselves make our world a different place, a better place than it was before we came.

It is one thing to choose between good and evil. It is another thing entirely to learn to distinguish between the impulses of a holy heart and the cravings of the self. Being a moral person and being a holy person — a fully developed spiritual person — are two different things. To be a spiritual person, a person intent on living in the presence of God, we need a light to guide us along the way.

The spiritual path is always a long one, often an obscure one. It is not so much a way as it is a direction. Like a lodestone, it magnetizes us, draws us beyond our self-centered selves to our deepest selves, our highest selves, our searching selves.

No two paths are really the same. Each of us goes our own personal way. Only the direction, the down-deep yearning to touch the stars beyond us and the ocean within us, is common to us all. Then the problem becomes finding the one who is best able to help us find the path in ourselves without denying us the right to make the path for ourselves.

The Buddhist sages are only too conscious of the delicate difference between driving a person and leading a person to the spiritual water within the pool of cosmic life we call the soul. The Buddhist story of how that happens is a sobering one:

> Once upon a time, when it was the custom for disciples to move in with a Zen master to be tutored in the practice of Zen, a master was approached by a disciple intent on learning to be a Zen master himself. The student knew that if the master agreed to tutor him, he could be attached to the teacher for years, learning not simply how he prayed but how he served tea and swept the floor and washed his begging bowl. It was a way of life he sought, not simply an introduction to the scriptures.
>
> But in this case, the master would not even catch the student's eye. He passed in and out of the house and gave the young man no notice at all. Not a sound. Not a nod. No discussion of the process. No encouraging word.
>
> So the young seeker decided to convince the master of his sincerity by taking his place outside the master's door to meditate. And he sat there. And he sat there. And he sat there. For days. For weeks. For months. Still the master ignored him.
>
> Winter came and the snows set in. Surely the master would see his sincerity now, take him into the house now, accept him as a pupil now.

But the master came and went, either totally unaware or callously uninterested in the presence of this meditating young man.

What could possibly move the master, prove to him the seriousness of the student, the thirst of his soul?

Then the student realized the one thing that might prove his willingness to give his entire being to the spiritual life. One day he cut off his arm, bowed, and presented it to the master.

Then the master realized the sincerity of the young man.

Then the master admitted the student as a pupil to his home.

At first glance, the story seems, at best, absurd. Even macabre. Certainly not spiritual at all. If anything, it seems to be a story about an arrogant teacher and a too-compliant student, both of whom are in great need of spiritual development. And why the violence? What kind of spirituality comes with self-mutilation? What kind of so-called spiritual practice is this?

But if we probe long enough, deep enough, thoughtfully enough, the real meaning of the story begins to emerge in the mist of the mind. Suddenly we begin to see that the question with which the master has presented the student is a painfully straightforward and contemporary one: What are we willing to cut off in our lives to be really spiritual people? What will we sacrifice to be more of what we really want to be? Or more to the point, what are we willing to add to our lives in order to become everything else we are meant to be? What is it that will make us more than conscious, more than willful, more than lustful for things, things, and more things, in order to breathe with the breath of God?

No, the spiritual life is not a theology course. It is far more than study. People can study theology for years and, in the end, have learned really nothing at all about God. Coming to know God is more than theory; it is experience. To learn about God we must examine carefully what it is in us that is stretching us beyond the confines of our paltry little selves. We must begin to ask what it takes to teem with the life of the universe, to move to the vibrations of the soul.

But to do that, the story implies, there is something else of which we must become aware: teachers too ready to tell us what to do may not have much to teach us about God at all. They may be far more intent on telling us what they themselves want us to do than on enabling us to find out what God wants us to do.

In the end, the spiritual life requires that we trust what God is doing inside of us as well as what is expected of us by the people, the systems, the leaders around us. Someday, you see, we will all be called to stand alone, validated only by the presence of God within us. Then it will be clear whether or not we are really spiritual people, people whose own souls have the word of God as the compass point by which they live or are only moralistic people who hide safely behind the norms set by others.

It takes time to become a spiritual adult. On the way, there is practice and ritual and asceticisms, self-denial and silence and the creation of sacred space and sacred time. All of these are important. None of them, not even all of them together, is enough to make a truly spiritual person.

The spiritual life has to do with learning to breathe in the Spirit of God and then breathing that same energy out — to others, wherever we are, whatever we are doing, with whomever we are.

The spiritual life is, eventually, a matter of melting into the mind of God and refusing to be deterred — no matter what institution says otherwise, no matter what institution wants less, no matter what institution demands more obeisance to itself than it does identity with the will of God.

It takes years of following the compass more than the rules. It means a lifetime of mistakes and spiritual failures and passing distractions, some of them even seemingly holy: fasts and prayers and moral evaluations of everyone we meet. Those are the real temptations against the spiritual life, more serious than sin, more pathetic than any amount of inattention, because they bear the risk that we ourselves might even consider ourselves holy.

Put more directly: wearing robes and saying prayers, learning to bow and keeping a schedule — important as such disciplines may be to the centering of the soul — are not the ultimate test of the spiritual life.

The monk Daruma spent nine years sitting in zazen facing a wall. So long and diligently did he practice sitting in meditation that his legs dropped off.

When the master came by, he said to Daruma, "What are you doing?"

And the monk said, "I'm practicing zazen so I may gain enlighten-ment."

The master frowned a minute, picked up a piece of pottery, and be-gan to rub it on his sleeve. The monk waited and waited but the master simply went on rubbing the piece of glaze.

Finally, unable to wait any longer, the monk said, "Master, what are you doing?"

"I'm making a mirror," the master said.

"You can't make a mirror like that!" the monk said incredulously.

"And you can't gain enlightenment simply sitting like that either," the master said.

The spiritual life is about more than the repetition of spiritual exer-cises. It demands commitment to discovering the essence of life. It requires the perseverance it takes to try and try again to find the way that is most life-giving for us — one community, one guide after another, if necessary, until we find ourselves truly alive spiritually, truly at home. It is about be-ing open to every moment, however incomplete, because every moment in life has something to teach us about what it means to live well. It is about realizing that sometimes the perfection of the moment lies in accepting its imperfections.

To this day, in Japan, they sell little Daruma dolls to remind seekers of what it means to live in a state of awareness. There are two types. One is a cylindrical paperweight that sits stolid and unmoving. The other has a round, weighted bottom. No matter how many times it is knocked over, it rebounds again. "Seven times down, eight times up," the saying goes. In-deed.

The meaning for the spiritual life is obvious: it is not spiritual prac-tices that define the value of our spiritual life. It is when we persist, perse-vere, go on and on and on until we become what we seek that we are really spiritual people.

To whom should we go to become spiritual people? Answer: to no one who, in the name of religion, orders us to be more a spiritual robot, less a spiritual person.

CHAPTER 9

What Does It Take to Succeed?

They were nice boys from a topsy-turvy kind of family: growing up, there had been too many children in too short a time. Then there was too much sickness, too much death, too little money. So there were no designer schools or good connections or special language tutors to depend on, like so many of the other boys in their school could take for granted. Instead, these boys made their own meals at night, played basketball on the street, and never saw the inside of the high-cost ski and tennis clubs that were all the rage of suburban USA in those days.

In the end, they all scraped by on their own steam and managed to graduate from high school regardless. Two worked their way through school and saved enough money to go on to college. The other two didn't go to college, but they were good, steady kids who kept a job, paid their bills, and moved on to corporation sandlot baseball teams. No one expected much more than decent, average survival from any of them.

Yet, one of the older boys retired to live off his investments before he was 40. The oldest son became a department supervisor of one of the largest financial organizations in the country by the time he was 45. The third son became an electrical engineer right out of college in a small local plant nobody ever heard of — or at least never expected to hear about again. By the time the plant got its first national contract, however, he and the owner were like father and son with all the privileges and future opportunities that implied.

Only the youngest son seemed to flounder a bit getting started at things. His grades in school were always only borderline. His interests never emerged quite as strong and clear as the others had. He didn't really know what he wanted to do in life, he said, and he didn't really seem to care that he didn't know. So he went into the armed forces out of high school "to give himself more time to decide."

For a while, it even looked as if he had finally found his career in America's peacetime army — by accident, if nothing else. He got good commendations, he was promoted once or twice, he wrote glowing letters home to his sick dad about his experiences and his work, simple as it seemed to be. He talked about reenlisting.

Then, out of nowhere it seemed, the crash came. He wandered away from the base. He failed to report for duty on time. He wound up in a brig. Over and over again, in the course of it all, he tried to tell people that he didn't "feel right," but the army medics gave him a clean bill of health, and the army brass put him under more and more pressure. By the time he showed up at his brother's house, he was talking back to the voices that plagued him.

After that, he wandered in and out of VA hospitals for years, never quite able to outrun the voices he heard, never able to completely ignore them.

The others all married lovely young women, bought beautiful houses, had gorgeous children, fit with aplomb into the suburbia they themselves had never known. The youngest brother's counselors, though, all discouraged him from marrying. And yet he was the gentlest, the most tender of them, the most vulnerable of them all. If anyone needed a companion through life, he did.

But there was no one, they said, that could ever be for him. It was better, they told him, that he not even think of marriage. "For lots of reasons," they put it. The reasoning was vague, perhaps, but the message was clear. So he did what few people ever really do: he became the panoptic companion for anyone and everyone else. He became the quiet presence in every family — the omnipresent uncle, the caretaker of the sick, the chauffeur for the aunt, the all-round available Kelly Boy for anyone who needed him. He spent life simply allowing himself to be taken for granted. He just was: he was there. He was caring. He was always available. He was the universal brother, uncle, son, friend. He was the silent but indispensable appendage to everybody else's life.

Some people might say that he was the only member of the family who was not able to succeed. They would be wrong. They would have confused success with prosperity or fame. Prosperity has something to do with an accumulation of things. Fame has to do with being noticed. Success has to do with becoming what we are supposed to be — fully developed human beings for whom life is a cache of experience, not a series of events.

Success is what we get when we embrace every dimension of life, lusting for none more than the others, rejecting none as less acceptable than the others, evaluating none as unimportant.

The Buddhist tradition gives us a model of success that far too many would call failure:

> Once upon a time, Tetsugen, a follower of Zen in Japan, decided to publish the sutras, the life of the Buddha, in Japanese. At that time the sutras were still available only in Chinese. To translate and publish these works in Japanese, then, would be a project of great significance, the value of which would be applauded everywhere.
>
> The books were to be printed with wood blocks in an edition of seven thousand copies, a tremendous undertaking.
>
> Tetsugen began by traveling and collecting donations for this purpose. A few sympathizers would give him a hundred pieces of gold, but most of the time he received only small coins. He thanked each donor with equal gratitude. Finally, after ten long years of begging, Tetsugen had enough money to begin his task.
>
> It happened that at that very time the Uji River overflowed. Famine followed. Tetsugen took the money he had collected to publish the books and gave it away to save the villagers on the river from starving to death.
>
> Then he began again his work of collecting the money necessary to produce the sutras.
>
> This time it took seven years before Tetsugen had enough money again to begin his task. But the money was barely collected before an ep-

idemic spread across the country. This time Tetsugen gave away what he had collected to help the sick.

After twenty more years of begging, he was at last able to publish the sutras in Japanese.

The printing blocks that produced the first edition of sutras can still be seen today in the Obaku monastery in Kyoto. But today the Japanese tell their children that Tetsugen made three sets of sutras, and that the first two invisible sets surpass even the last one.

The model of success we get here is, by and large, a foreign one to a modern world.

The story makes a point that contemporary society has been long inclined to forget: there are standards of success that no amount of achievement can possibly equal. In a world that counts achievement in terms of dollars and houses and titles, it is maintaining standards of success based more on values than on things that is the most difficult task of all.

When success is equated in things, it goes when the things go, even when the things are called sacred. If we value going to church more than living the faith, then when the church closes, the faith dies, too, and we do not succeed spiritually.

If we value social connections more than we value a relationship with our children, then when we fade from the social scene, we abandon old friends and fail as parents, as well.

If we value money more than we value the work we do, then when the money we get for doing the work is not what we want it to be, we jettison the work and our gifts along with it. Then, when the flood comes in whatever form — in the form of a job loss or a failed test or economic embarrassment, in the form of physical disability or social disfigurement or emotional breakdown — our sense of personal success goes with it. We hide our faces — even from ourselves. We collapse inside. We lose faith. Our backbones crumble and stoop us.

Then it is time to consider again what a successful life really looks like. If it's about achievement, what have we achieved that will last beyond the power to rust or break or steal it? What have we achieved that is within our own power to maintain — like a love of good music, the memory of two poems, a favorite story? Is there anyone who loves us enough to go on laughing with us when the losses come? Most of all, do we really love anyone besides ourselves?

A world built on prestige and social status has distorted the very idea of success. It is not what we have done that is important. It is whether or not anything we did was worth doing. Worth it for someone else, that is. Worth it for those who are starving or homeless or sick today.

The ancient masters ask us one of the bedrock questions of life: To what invisible sutras have we given our lives? What great ideas live on in us, shine out through us, have voice through us?

When people look back and ask what we achieved in life, what it was to which we gave our hearts, will there be only a property list, a membership list, and a bank balance to show for it? Or will there, perhaps, be one starving, one homeless, one sick, one spiritually lost, one lonely person standing there who can say, in our behalf, that if we had not lived, their own life would have been much poorer?

There is no doubt that we will succeed. The only question is, In what? It's not the things we do that count in the end. It's the way we do the things we must do that makes the difference.

We can all spend our lives on the sutras, the holy books of our choice, and never live them. In which case, they, too, will begin to pale in value, thanks to us.

Did all the boys in that little family of misfortune and struggle succeed? Indeed, they did. Perhaps most of all, the youngest son, the one whose life looks so devoid of what the rest of us have been taught to call "achievement." He succeeded, first and foremost, as a human being in a situation in which many of us may not have done nearly so well. In his life, we read the invisible print of visible struggle crowned by the kind of success so easily surrendered in the pursuit of lesser kinds of fortune.

CHAPTER 10

Is It Possible to Make Up for Past Mistakes?

She sat across from me in the crowded little office, but huddled far back into the corner of the couch. Her legs were tightly crossed, her elbows against her ribs, one hand half-covering her face. She turned her body away from mine, her eyes down. I never doubted for a moment that whatever she had come to talk about was still as yet unsaid.

She was young, married only a few years, very nicely dressed — a little too nicely dressed for a private office visit at mid-week, I thought — but very business-like. She finally began to talk a bit, but the words had no ring of truth or urgency to them. Her husband lacked ambition, she said. He had no goals, as she did, beyond what he was already doing. He didn't care about the intellectual dimensions of the field.

She, on the other hand, she told me, wanted to do research, maybe get a position in a university. He was simply willing to stay where he was, seeing very pedestrian clients in a very workaday office, day after day after day. She didn't know how she could go on like that. But there were already two children. So she also didn't know how she could leave. And? I said. And?

And, she finally whispered hoarsely, she was deeply involved with someone else. Someone she was meeting after work and on weekends and on any pretense whatsoever. Someone who, ironically, loved fishing and hiking and walking in the woods. Someone who had no career at all, apparently. Someone with whom she could laugh and forget her professional self and its concerns about success. Someone who brought humor and daring and freedom to her and to whom she had become a kind of mythical Pygmalion figure. This relationship she could mold as she chose rather than be required to partner through the fine art of dailiness.

The problem? She could not leave the marriage, but she could not relinquish the other person either. Her agony was plain to see. Her husband loved her and she knew it. More than that, she loved him, too. He was good. He was steady. He was gentle. Maybe too good, too steady, too predictable at a time when she needed some excitement and wanted some relief from small children and daily routine.

The temptation in a situation like that, of course, is to press a person to make a decision: Clean it up. Get it over with. Do what's right. Don't dally. Don't court danger. Do it right now and for your own good.

But decisions made under pressure are seldom ever really decisions. Instead, they come back to haunt us in a myriad of ways: as regret, as anger, as depression. "Think it over," I said. "Forever is a long time."

After a while, the time between appointments lengthened and then, after a few well-spaced calls, stopped entirely.

When she finally came back to see me again, months later, a new agony had replaced the old one. The secret relationship had finally petered off into a distant but amicable friendship. The marriage never suffered from the woman's own private emotional upheaval and was, she reported, even better than before. But now guilt ate away at her like fine acid, like bitter herbs. To tell him, to confess, to wail at his feet, she felt, would only forever destroy the trust between them. Not to tell him left her alone carrying a burden she could never put down. Now, she said, she simply could not live with herself, forgive herself, unburden herself of the betrayal for which she was secretly punishing herself.

Was there no way to make up for this interruption of the ordinary that could, if revealed now, destroy them in a way the secret intrigue had never been able to do? It was one thing to resolve the affair; it had become entirely another to resolve the guilt that dogged at her heels ever since. The affair was over, but the price to be paid for it had just begun to dawn.

GUILT — normal, balanced, healthy guilt, guilt without pretense and without neurotic exaggeration — is the mark of a basically good and decent person who has failed to meet their own ideals. This is the kind of guilt that seeks repair. But how?

How do we fix, without doing even more damage, what in some cases never even looked broken? How do we make up, even to ourselves, for what has been damaged, if not in the other, at least in ourselves? Like a crack in crystal, it is always there, just enough to mar the perfection of the glass, never enough to shatter it completely. It says only too clearly, "I am not what I want people to think I am. What I look like is not what I know myself to be." How do I repair damage that no one even knows has been done but that goes to every mirror with me, day and night, eating away at my image of my self?

And therein lies the key: "repair" is repair; it is not replacement. Something is always different after it has been repaired. The dent is gone, perhaps, but the color of the piece, for instance, is also just slightly deeper, or darker, or thinner than before. And yet, it is also, in a way, new again, too. It has had another beginning, another point from which to mark its wear, another moment after which things can be different, can even be stronger than they were before.

Once that moment comes, the task is to accept the newness of the thing, not to mourn the mistakes of the past. It is a matter of becoming whole again. I may be forever sorry that a thing has happened, but I cannot be forever paralyzed by it. Life goes on, and so must this relationship, so must I, and in whole new ways.

In Buddhist philosophy, karma — the notion that behavior has consequences, that the goal of life is to "make merit," to practice doing good so that good can follow — is basic and never impossible. There is no such thing, to the Buddhist, as eternal damnation.

Failure, to the Buddhist, is not the end of us and all the good we've ever done. It is not necessarily destructive at all unless we choose to wallow in the pit we have made for ourselves, to cease striving, to forget to begin again. On the contrary. If we stumble, our one obligation is to get up and start over. In fact, if the damage we have done is not satisfied in this life, it can be satisfied in the next. What we do not do in this life, Buddhism reminds us, we can, if we will, repair now or carry into the next life until we do.

The sages tell a story that is clear on the point:

Zenkai, the son of a samurai, journeyed to Edo and there became the retainer of a high official. He fell in love with the official's wife and was discovered. To save himself, he slew the official and then ran away with the wife.

Both of them later became thieves. But the woman was so greedy that Zenkai grew disgusted. Finally, leaving her, he journeyed far away to the province of Buzen where he became a wandering mendicant.

To atone for his past, Zenkai resolved to accomplish some good deed in his lifetime. Knowing of a dangerous road over a cliff that had caused the death and injury of many persons, he resolved to cut a tunnel through the mountain there.

Begging food in the daytime, Zenkai worked at night digging his tunnel. When thirty years had gone by, the tunnel was 2,280 feet long, 20 feet high, and 30 feet wide.

Two years before the work was completed, the son of the official he had slain, who was a skillful swordsman, found Zenkai out and came to kill him in revenge.

"I will give you my life willingly," said Zenkai. "Only let me finish this work. On the day it is completed, then you may kill me."

So the son awaited the day. Several months passed, and Zenkai kept on digging. The son grew tired of doing nothing and began to shovel himself. After he had helped for more than a year, realizing now how difficult and demanding the work had been, he came to admire Zenkai's strong will and character.

At last the tunnel was completed and the people could travel in safety.

"Now you can cut off my head," said Zenkai. "My work is done."

"How can I cut off my own teacher's head?" said the younger man. And the tears were flowing down his face.

It's a story about repentance, of course, but it is also a story about forgiveness. To see a person so completely converted, so much a model of what it means to give back to society what they have taken from it, and to destroy them because of their past, would be, the son realizes, a crime in itself.

What the son learns from Zenkai, and will someday surely need himself, is the fine art of starting over in life. He sees that it is possible to change. Whatever we have been, we can change. Whatever we have done, we can repent. Whatever we have destroyed, we can undo, if not in coin at least in kind. Whatever we want to become as a person, we may.

Life is a process made up of many experiments, many mistakes, many learnings, many possibilities. Sometimes it is only error that can possibly teach us the value of goodness or show us the path to our own growth.

Our own great sins help us to understand two things in life: how easy it is to allow ourselves to sink into moral nothingness; and how little it takes to be a decent human being.

What we are in the end is the sum of what we have learned from everything we have done in the past.

Beware the rigid. They are afraid of life and trust nothing and no one because they long ago learned not to trust themselves. They judge everyone else by their own past errors. Self-centered to the utmost, they have decided that if they, who are the center of the universe, have erred, no one else can possibly do better. Rigidity is simply another kind of pride. It ends in suspicion, judgmentalism, and hardness of heart. Their moral pride insists that all the Zenkai's in the world must be killed for their crimes, even long after they have repented them.

Beware the amoral, as well. They make no distinction whatsoever between good and bad, better and worse. They may look like people of quality because they are never seen sinning. But they have few convictions by which to steer their lives. They go with the wind, judging no one, true, least of all themselves, but little prepared to explain to another the moral compass by which they steer their lives. As a result, their witness to a kind of cosmetic goodness has little value to the human community.

The truth is that we grow into goodness by being good to others, by being willing to start over again ourselves every time we do less than the world deserves and decency demands. The Buddhist would say that bad actions have bad consequences, good actions have good consequences. Determining how we want to be in the world — a person because of whom good consequences come or a person who cares little about the effects of an action — makes all the difference.

Life shapes us as we go. No one is born perfect; no one dies that way. Along the path of life, great ideals often come face-to-face with great personal cravings and intense human impulses. Then we struggle between human possibility and human shame. Then regret, guilt, can consume us, stop us in our tracks, discourage and defeat us. Or guilt, remorse, can drive us to be more than we were before — wiser in the ways of greatness, more steadfast in the ways of goodness that undo macroscopically the bad consequences of the past.

If the question is, Is it possible to make up for past mistakes? the answer must be that it is always possible. How else can we explain that so many great saints — so many of whose lives slogged and sloshed through the dregs of life — began as great sinners?

Regret and guilt are two great graces of life. The key is to get up every morning determined to leave more good in my wake than pain.

Jewish Community

CHAPTER 11

Where Did I Lose My Idealism?

I hadn't seen Dan for years — for so long, in fact, that I had to look twice and then again before I recognized him. It wasn't that he had aged. On the contrary, he was more handsome than I had ever known him in those earlier years. Now his tight, dark, curly hair had a flare to the cut of it. The white shirt collar was stiff with starch. And the tie was silk. No doubt about it — silk. That was the real difference.

The last time I'd seen Dan he had long hair that hung down over the collar of his cotton polo shirt. His blue jeans were frayed around the pockets. He never wore a white shirt in those days, and he didn't know what a tie was.

I caught myself just before the delight of recognition on my face could turn to incredulity. "Dan, how wonderful to see you again," I said. "What are you doing *here?*" "Here," I realized after I'd said it, had the slightest touch of amazement to it. Here was corporate USA. I could have imagined Dan in a youth hostel, of course, or a soup kitchen, maybe, or even in a classroom. But here, in the finance office of a small college in a small town in rural Republican territory? Hardly.

It was a good job, a very decent thing to do, but so unlike anything Dan had ever wanted to do. If anything, he had come late to such propriety.

When I first met Dan, he was on his way to Washington to be part of a major peace demonstration. Then he had gone off to protest U.S. militarism at what was then called The School of the Americas, a U.S. military training school in Georgia. Dan, then a professional peacenik, said that the place was used to train foreign military in guerilla warfare and "investigative" techniques — otherwise called "torture" when other countries did it. Over the years, he had risked arrest there annually.

After that Dan lived in a commune for awhile, then drifted out to the Midwest and simply disappeared. No Christmas cards. No phone calls. No sudden visits on the way through to the next Quixotic attempt to call the world back from the brink of its own destruction.

"Have you been able to get to any of the Pax Christi Assemblies lately?" I asked, trying to rekindle old memories. There was the slightest hint of a blush on his cheek, I thought, as he answered me. "No," he said, "I don't do any of that anymore. You know, here," he waved his hand across the campus landscape and shrugged a bit, "those things aren't much of an issue."

Nor were those issues of much concern now for Dan either, it seemed. Somehow Dan had moved on in life, moved away from the ideas that had once been the lodestone of his life to quieter, safer, more socially acceptable involvements. He had, I suppose some would say, "grown up." He had at least grown beyond those early moments of awareness and commitment to a kind of fledged resignation, perhaps, or even disillusionment, maybe.

Whatever the situation, it is not an uncommon one. Most of us moderate our hopes and sureties along the way. Whatever our early passions, in the long run we get "reasonable." Or, if not reasonable, definitely resigned to life "the way it is." We simply give up. We come to know, finally, that what we spent so much young energy working for is simply not going to happen. Sometimes we even come to doubt that it should.

Idealism, of all the energies of the soul, may be one of its most vulnerable. Nothing else within us gives in so easily to failure, to rationalism, to doubt — not love, not anger, not ambition. Love persists in the face of rejection, often to the point of foolishness. Anger refuels itself time and time again, even when the coals that once flamed have been apparently extinguished. Ambition eats at the soul long after the opportunities disappear or all hope of achievement is lost. The slightest breeze of recollection serves to reignite them all. But it's different with idealism.

Because it is bred more by vision than by likelihood, idealism gives way, it seems, to one of two things. Either there is a rigid return to past commitments: "The hawks are right: peace is not possible." Or it sinks into a kind of hollow desperation, to resignation without reward of hope — or hope of reward: "You know, those things aren't much of an issue here."

Idealism, the spirit that leads a person to believe that the world can be better, that things can change, that a new time must come, is hydroponic. It does not grow naturally without help. It must be nurtured by the very spirit it cherishes. Not simply because I want it will something better happen, but only because I go on believing that there is a best in the human condition, even at its worst. The world will change because it must change. The best simply cannot not be. Idealism is bred by idealism.

Jewish spirituality teaches that if we live a righteous life long enough we will eventually come to be as righteous as we look. It never doubts the need to go on when going on seems least likely to succeed. Where many criticize the whole notion of religion done by rote, the Jewish community simply assumes that if we do a thing often enough we will eventually become what we do. "The heart is drawn after the deeds," the rabbis say. The message is clear: if we do a thing long enough, eventually we'll get it. If we keep practicing, we'll eventually understand, eventually grasp the necessity of it. If we go on long enough, eventually we'll take going on for granted. We will internalize the meaning of it until the action and the idea are one in us and we in it. Then we will learn to decline to be disillusioned, refuse to be discouraged, insist on going on whether "it's an issue here" or not. But, the rabbis also know, the welding of the two is not the only possibility. It is not the only thing that can happen, and it does not always happen. Why? Because just as actions can change the heart, it is also true that the heart must be open to more than simply the actions themselves.

In the face of such impractical idealism — the notion that I can become what I believe simply by acting like I believe it often enough — even the most committed traditionalist, the most adamant pragmatist is forced to think again. The Jewish tradition enshrines the broader worldview in story:

> Once upon a time, a young rabbi, Rabbi Shalom, happened to be traveling through a small town in the district of Kiev and asked for hospitality at the house of the local rabbi. The old zaddik Rabbi Zev had al-

ready arrived at home to spend the Sabbath there. On Thursday evening, the night before Shabbat, Rabbi Shalom prepared to leave and went to bid Rabbi Zev farewell. The zaddik inquired when Rabbi Shalom expected to reach his destination. "Tomorrow, around three in the afternoon," the rabbi said.

"Why do you plan to be on the road after noon hour on the day the Sabbath begins?" Rabbi Zev asked in surprise. "At twelve o'clock I usually put on my Sabbath clothes and start singing the 'Song of Songs,' which is Solomon's. By that time the Sabbath peace has already begun for me."

"And what am I to do," replied Rabbi Shalom, "if a tenant farmer comes to me toward evening and tells me his troubles, tells me that his calf has fallen sick, and from his words I gather that he is saying to me: 'You are a lofty soul, and I am a lowly soul; lift me up to you!' What am I to do then?"

From off the table the old rabbi took two candlesticks with the lighted candles, and grasping them in his two hands, he accompanied his young guest through the long corridor to the outer door. "Go in peace," he said. "Go in peace."

The story pierces the heart of the perfect with the hint of an even more perfect world. For those who want to be perfect rather than holy, the rules are enough. For those who want to be holy even if they cannot be perfect, only the ideal, only what ought to be is enough. Investing myself in the Sabbath is one thing, the story implies. Investing every last minute of my life, right up to the edge of the Sabbath, in the needs of the other, the story argues back, is entirely another. One is Sabbath practice; the other is the very ideal of messianic presence of which the Sabbath speaks to us.

It is so easy to sink back into the rules of life, as the old rabbi has done over the years. We can even begin to take comfort in them. Once we make peace with less than the ideal, we begin to make virtue out of the routine of ritual, out of the customary. However far from the ideal it may be, it can begin to look like the ideal to us if for no other reason than that everyone around us thinks it is.

Rabbi Shalom, on the other hand, the young rabbi, is clearly an idealist. Unlike Rabbi Zev, who takes no chances of violating the Sabbath by being on the road as the sun goes down and Sabbath begins, Rabbi Shalom is intent on being where he might be needed before the sun sets. He risks the violation of the Sabbath for the sake of the people he serves.

Rabbi Zev, on the other hand, has long ago begun to put more energy into the Sabbath — even hours before Sabbath really begins — than into the people. He puts on special clothes. He begins to sing Sabbath songs. He substitutes liturgy for availability to the people. He has convinced himself that perfect celebration of the Sabbath is the full measure of his dedication, of his holiness, of his life.

But Rabbi Shalom, young as he may be, knows the difference between celebrating the Sabbath and living the Torah.

Shimon the Righteous says: "The world stands on three things: on Torah, on worship, and on acts of loving kindness." On a tripod, perfectly balanced, one leg does not eclipse the others. Rabbi Zev has come to perch on ritual. But Rabbi Shalom, a Jew who knows the fullness of the Torah, is as much dedicated to doing acts of loving kindness as he is to meeting the particulars of worship.

Rabbi Shalom worships God by serving the people of God as well as by concentrating on the Sabbath. And the tradition defends him for it. Study, the Talmud teaches, should be combined with worldly concerns. "Those who do not do this," the rabbis say, "are as if they have no God."

Rabbi Shalom wants something far more than the outward symbols of the inward life. He is intent on bringing all three elements of Judaism into play, whatever the risk to his own purity of life, his own spiritual security, his own obligations to worship. It is a rare and brazen attitude. The people look to us, he implies to Rabbi Zev, to help them bear their real burdens, not simply to light our own candles in peace.

Then the old man, carrying the candles that are the very sign of Sabbath, the signal of that move from mundane affairs to sacred affairs, conducts Shalom to the door, Sabbath candles blazing. In Rabbi Shalom, the old man knows — in Shalom's linking of the ceremonial with the real, in his idealism — the spirit of Sabbath has really arrived.

We all find it easy to retreat from the ideal to the acceptable. It is so much more secure, more comfortable, to know that we have kept the rules, done religion right, walked in the ways of the world's social graces rather than risked the pitfalls of the prophet.

We lose a piece of our idealism every time we choose to follow the rules of a society rather than its ideals. Every time we seek approval rather than understanding, rather than possibility, we close down another part of our souls. We begin to do what is safe rather than what is holy. We start to defend what is acceptable rather than insist on what is necessary — for the poor, for the globe — so that the institution can be what it says it is.

Dan is doing well, I hear. Dan, I'm sure, is even doing good. Whether or not he is doing what needs to be done, saying what needs to be said, asking what needs to be asked is another question. Those things take courage. Those things take enormous spiritual effort. Those things take immense resilience. To keep coming back to say, Why not? in the face of a world that says only "Because" — because it has always been this way; because that's the way things are; because it would take too much money to do it otherwise; because I said so — is exhausting. It can even be maddening. It can certainly be depressing. But it can never be useless.

In all of us there is the voice of the young rabbi, Shalom, wanting to be heard. In all of us, too, there is the soul of the old rabbi, Zev, trying to remember what it is like to be more married to the ideal than to the institution that pretends to enshrine it.

Where did we lose our idealism? In our hunger for approval. How can we revive it? By refusing to ignore the cries of the people for the sake of the system, by refusing, always, to be silent.

CHAPTER 12

Why Do I Feel Stuck?

It isn't that he wasn't bright enough. Nonsense. He was one of the smartest people I'd ever met. He had had years of academic success. He had a fine reputation as a teacher. He certainly had the right pedigree: a professional family, an elite university career, a good doctorate from the right department, a list of good publications.

But whatever the cosmetics, he was never really happy — always dissatisfied, always stuck, always wanting more. What he was, it seems, never quite equaled his image of himself and what he wanted to be. Shakespeare, in one of his sonnets, had described the type centuries ago. He was forever "desiring this one's art and that one's scope." It wasn't so much that other people discounted him. It was that he was never good enough for himself.

Standing next to him, you could almost feel the restless rage that ate away at his soul.

He carried an air of perpetual disdain, a kind of groundless anger, at those who refused to recognize in him what he thought himself to be. He hungered for the world to attest that he was what he clearly was not.

He was even angrier at those who had the recognition he craved and were clearly what he wanted to be.

He was stuck. He could not be what he wanted to be. He did not want to be what he was, however excellent that might look to others. Instead, he drifted between the two, unhappy because of what he could not do, refusing to be satisfied with what he could do. But the wanting ate him up, consumed him, made him small when he could have been great.

As a result, his career, good as it was, never really reached the professional heights most people would have expected. He didn't want to be a teacher; he wanted to be an administrator. He didn't want to be a theorist; he wanted to be an executive. And he never got to be either.

If truth were known, he had a great need to be both powerful and popular, to be the dashing center of the system. He wanted to be liked. He also wanted to be chief, head, top of the heap. But that is a rare combination. "Charismatic," they call it, "an extraordinary ability to attract." That he did not have.

At the same time, he was without doubt an invaluable resource on anybody's committee, on anybody's staff, on anybody's board. But what he definitely did not want to be was one of the team — any team. He wanted to be the standout best so he could eclipse the best in everyone else. He wanted all the light on himself. He wanted to consume all the air in the room.

Instead, he became a study of what happens when we reject parts of ourselves and leave the whole of ourselves untouched, undeveloped. We miss one of the major lessons of nature: just because turkeys do not fly long distances does not make them failed birds.

FAILING TO BECOME what we want to be, we refuse to be the best that we are.

But why do we do it? What is there in us that refuses to face the circumstances of life — who we are, what we can do, where we are most valuable — and then do something to make it a happy place to be for ourselves?

There is, of course, the rescue mentality spawned in the fairytale stages of life. We sit and wait for someone else to make us happy. We demand that the world save us from ourselves. We expect that there will be a magic sword or a knight in shining armor that will free us from our present condition and simply supply us with the life we deserve. We expect other people to take responsibility for our unhappiness. They should protect us or elect us or do something to crown us — and when they don't, we wilt.

But rescue is not a likely scenario in a world where people come and go out of our lives now in rapid succession. There are few who remain forever anymore. So there are few who know us well enough or stay with us long enough to rescue us, even if they could. People stake their directions early now and move on to follow them. Schoolmates disappear into their own lives. Work groups change with amazing rapidity in a global society. We ourselves follow the yellow brick road wherever it leads, taking one position after another until we run out of professional options. Even the counselors we pay to help us hear ourselves, to help us find ourselves in the rubble of our disappointments, are likely to shift from place to place. Rescue is clearly an unlikely source of happiness now.

So, what is it that stops us from accepting who we are?

Sometimes it's the Great Imposter syndrome. Sometimes we convince even ourselves that we are who we say we are. The problem with posing is that it dooms us to failure. When we say we can do what we clearly are not prepared to do, we walk naked through life fearing to be seen. Taking on more than we can do is a high-wire act without benefit of a net. One misstep and there is no hope of success again.

Sometimes it's fear of being found out. Sometimes the bluster we have for so long learned to affect manages to really convince us that we are who we want to be. If we admit to someone that we know we're not, what will they think of us?

What's best? An honest awareness of our best possibilities or the faint hope that people will go on thinking we could be more than we are — if only we ever got a chance to be it? If we go on pretending long enough, even to ourselves, wouldn't it surely happen? And even if it doesn't, isn't it better to be thought capable of something we want to do — and martyred by rejection — than to have it known that we are not capable of doing more than we are?

The problem with all those strategies is that none of them can possibly succeed. We cannot be what we are not. We can only become the whole of what we are, and learn to accept it, and learn to enjoy being it.

One thing we can do is to begin to go about life differently. Life is not one thing only. No one's life is totally one-dimensional. We are all a great deal more than the world knows us to be. So when one dimension of life fails to work for us, we can take all of who we are and become what we must some other way.

We can learn how to treat ourselves with the respect we are struggling to get from others. We ourselves must accept what we are if we want other people to value it, too. Instead of trying to be what we are not, we must become the best, the happiest, of what we are. People are attracted to happiness, not to anger or disdain or resentment or negativity or jealousy.

It is the ability to spread happiness that moves the world, that gives a person scope, that makes a person desirable, that unsticks me from the obsession on which I'm stuck.

Jewish spirituality speaks to the situation with an insight that is both humorous and enlightening:

> Once when the Jews were passing through a period of great stress, the Rabbi of Apt, who was then the eldest of his generation, issued a command for a universal fast in order to call down God's mercy.
>
> But Rabbi Israel, another rabbi in the area, took a different approach. He summoned his musicians, whom he carefully selected from a number of different towns. Night after night he had them play their most beautiful melodies on the balcony of his house.
>
> Whenever the sound of the clarinet and the delicate tinkle of the little bells floated down from above, all the Jews in the territory began to gather in the garden until there was a whole crowd of them. The music would soon triumph over their dejection and they would dance, stamping their feet and clapping their hands.
>
> People who were indignant at these doings reported to the Rabbi of Apt that the day of fasting he had ordered had been turned into a day of rejoicing. But he answered them, "It is not up to me to call him to account who has kept the memory of the command in the scriptures green in his heart. The scripture says, 'And when you go to war in your land against the adversary that oppresseth you, then ye shall sound an alarm with the trumpets. And you shall be remembered before the Lord your God.'"

The story is a simple one. Doing what we can do in every situation, doing it well, and doing it with joy is not only good for us but is good for those around us as well. The two rabbis in the story are very different people. They go about the same work of life in very different ways. And they are both effective, both revered. Each of them has a gift of his own to give. For one of them to try to be the other would not only fail but would deprive the world of the fullness of human gifts.

God does not want us to be paralyzed in the face of difficulty. God does not listen more to the dour than to the joyful. God wants us to have the faith to know that whatever our gifts, whoever we are, we can deal with whatever we face in life with a trusting heart because we know that God is with us, too.

We don't have to get stuck in the dregs of life. We don't have to pine away wanting to be what we are not. We don't have to doubt that our gifts are fit or will be received. We don't have to wonder if what we have to give the world is worth giving.

But we do have to do something positive with the gifts we do have or risk the loss of them entirely.

Rabbi Israel refused to be stuck. He knew what he could do and he accepted, as well, what others brought to the situation. He did not see himself as the whole of the solution, but he realized that he was part of it. He knew that there is always another way to go about the difficult dimensions of life, even when it seems that there is nothing whatsoever different that we can do about it.

We can, of course, simply change our attitude. We can realize that what we have within us is the best gift we have to give. And we can give it joyfully.

Or we can do what we do — however limited we are in it right now — because that is the way life is at this moment, but do something else, as well. Coming home from a bad job and going to bed angry does not enable me to change anything about the job. But I can change what I do when I go home. I can take the time to learn to paint, for instance. I can teach myself to restore furniture and start a small business on the side. I can begin a weekly pizza-and-beer discussion group. I can begin to play cards and create a circle of friends who are also learning to play the other music of their lives.

It's either that or spend my life simply singing its dirges for what I cannot be rather than learning to rejoice in what I can be — and what I am called to be.

We are not meant to get stuck in life. We are meant to go on from layer to layer of our souls until we get to the core of the spiritual life and find faith in all of it.

We are meant to sing our way from one thing to another in life so that we can come to know the blessings of life, of God, in every dimension.

Why am I stuck in life? Easy. If I am stuck it is because I am refusing to move on beyond my jealousies and unrealistic yearnings, to take life as it is, to develop what I am and to find my own music in it until I simply cannot stop myself from becoming my own song.

CHAPTER 13

What Can I Do
When Enough Is Enough?

I'd been in the Far East before, but never like this. Most of my trips to Asia had been for conferences in Catholic monasteries or to attend events in Buddhist monasteries. In China, for public events, we were conducted through the city on a carefully guarded visitors' route. In Japan, the meetings were held in one of those astonishing empty rooms that the Japanese are so famous for: a vase with one flower here, a wall-size tapestry in deep, dark colors there. Nothing but space and soft colors to soothe the soul. In the temples we visited on the mountainsides, there was just emptiness and awesome statues of the Buddha thirty feet high.

In Taiwan, however, the visit took a different turn. The old Japanese Zen temple in which we stayed had been turned into a conference center with wide staircases and dark halls. Each room had a patio overlooking the garden. The ceilings were two stories high. Inside, during the day, in other words, everything felt open and calming, formal and monastic.

But then one evening everything changed. We left the old temple conference center and went to what Asians know as "the night market," a ticky-tacky string of wooden stalls that run for blocks on both sides of the narrow streets, full of small boutiques. Blinking neon lights on the rooftops above the lean-to booths flashed against the walls of the buildings behind them, punctuating the night with a kind of stinging frenzy. Boom boxes roared in every tiny entranceway. I could feel the cacophony, otherworldly and unremitting, vibrate to the very center of my system. To talk to one another about styles or to vendors about prices, my colleagues and I shouted at one another above the caterwaul of the noise around us or mouthed directions and pointed around corners as we wandered out of one narrow back street into another. Every block became less and less interesting to me.

By the time we got to the dark end of the market, my nerves were on fire and I could feel the tightness in my chest. I pushed my way through the crowd out onto the street and stepped in front of a barely slowing cab. In fact, I would have done anything by then to find sanctuary from the heat and the jangle, the smell and the jostle of this never-ending crowd. Here in this one place, on this long narrow byway, I thought, was all the population of the world. And it was too much. Forget the family gifts. Forget the sightseeing. Forget the bargaining. Just get me out of here.

The problem wasn't that I had had "enough" of it. I had had way too much of it. The noisy, pulsing crowd, the haggling, pressing vendors were all affecting me both mentally and physically. It was not enjoyable; it was overload, pure and simple, after days of travel, days of meetings. They call it stress.

But it is not peculiar to Taiwan. We are all living with more than we can handle now, one way or another, here as well as there. So what is it, and is it all bad? When is enough of it enough? And what, if any of it, is holy?

If you rub the thumb of one hand up and down on the other hand from the root of your finger to the back of your wrist, that's not stress. If you rub your thumb up and down from the root of your finger to the back of your wrist for one straight hour, that is. The skin begins to break down, to get inflamed, to swell a little, to break. It isn't that rubbing the back of one hand with the thumb of the other is wrong. In fact, massage therapists do it with great therapeutic effect. Your mistake is that you should have stopped rubbing it much sooner than you did.

Too much of anything in too great a dosage is stress. Too much traffic for too many hours a day for too many days a year is stress. Too much pressure, too much fatigue, too much debt, too much worry is stress. Too much of anything, in fact, is stress.

But stress itself is not necessarily bad. It takes a good deal of stress to do the creative, backbreaking work of meeting deadlines, writing papers, building a house, painting the living room. But, in most instances, that kind of stress is time-bound. If it has to be done by a certain day and hour, it probably will be, however incomplete. A due date becomes what stops us from spending our lives doing something that can be done in far less time and ought not to consume a life in the first place. Work that is limited, periodic, or confined to a certain time or place moves us from one thing to another in life, helping us to measure ourselves every step of the way.

Many of us don't even begin to do our best work unless there is a due date or a time test to meet. The closer the end-date to a project the harder we work, the more concentrated is our thinking, the faster our hearts beat, the more focused are our energies.

Obviously, stress can be a senseless burden as well as a good gift. When it wears us down physically, it limits what we ought to be doing with the strength we have. When it wears us down emotionally, it affects the way we respond to other people and pollutes their lives as well. When it wears us down psychologically, it confuses our reactions and befuddles the mind.

The point is that stress can be both positive and negative. But in the end, it has something to do with whether we turn our life into a living flame or burn it quickly down to black ash.

Stress is good or bad, holy or unholy, depending on how we cope with it, how we define it, how we allow it into our lives. Most interesting of all, perhaps, is that, contrary to what contemporary psychology would have us think, stress is not peculiar to this culture. We did not invent stress. We will not be able to eliminate it. All we can do is remember that learning how to respond to the pressures under which we live has always been one of the great aims of the spiritual life. Should we seek to escape them, or should we seek to control them? Is it holier to ignore them or to seek them in some kind of sacrificial overwork or burdensome pieties? Does sanctity require that we abandon ourselves to the tensions in which we find ourselves, accept them in a spirit of self-sacrifice, give ourselves over to their control, or learn how to live with the pressures that arise around us in the very process of living?

When the baby cries through the night and the children run screaming through the house from dawn to dusk and the deadline duties fall on your desk and the bills come in and the car breaks down and the arguments start and the supper burns, what is the spiritual answer then? Jewish spirituality is clear. "When hard things happen," the Rabbi of Kobryn taught, "do not say, 'That's bad, that's bad.' Nothing God imposes is bad. But it is all right to say: 'That's bitter,' for there are, indeed, some medicines made with bitter herbs."

The rabbi makes a point: there is something to be gained in stress, too. It is only a matter of learning to know when enough is enough.

Once upon a time, according to the tales of the Hasidim, Rabbi Israel joined the disciples, pipe in hand. It was a good time to ask a question.

"Tell us, dear rabbi," they said, "how should we serve God?"

The rabbi was surprised at the question but then began at once to tell them this story:

"There were two friends, and both were accused of a crime before the king. Since he loved them, he wanted to show them mercy. He could not acquit them because even the king's word cannot prevail over a law. So he gave this verdict:

"A rope was to be stretched across a deep chasm, and the two accused were to walk it, one after the other. Whosoever reached the other side was to be granted his life.

"It was done as the king ordered, and the first of the friends got safely across.

"The other, still standing in the same spot, cried to him: 'Tell me, my friend, how did you manage to cross this terrible chasm on that thin and swaying rope?'

"The first of the two prisoners called back: 'I don't know anything but this: whenever I felt myself toppling over to one side, I leaned to the other.'"

Rabbi Israel makes two points. First, no one solves the pressures of life simply by standing still. When life is off balance, the only way to stay on our feet is by moving in the other direction. Standing still — going on doing what we've been doing — only intensifies the tilt we're in.

Second, any excess — leaning either entirely to the right or entirely to the left — will only damage us one way or the other in the end. Extremes are not the answer to anything. Stopping everything leaves us without a sense of purpose, the heartbeat of our lives, a reason to get up in the morning. On the other hand, doing more of the same or doing it faster — even in an attempt to end the pressure — only hastens the burnout or the breakdown.

The answer to pressure and stress is not the death of the self from doing either too much or too little. It is life lived between the poles of too much and too little. It is life flavored by many things, not surfeited in any single thing that consumes our energies and dampens our appetite for the rest of life.

The spirituality of balance has five attributes: equilibrium, variety, self-awareness, re-creation, and an appreciation of the value of imperfection.

Equilibrium is the ability to know when to quit. When we find ourselves immersed in any one part of life to the detriment of all its other facets — family, prayer, rest, education, play — we are no longer running our lives; our lives are running us. Something we need, something that is air and blood to our very beings, is being denied. Something inside of us is drying up and will surely come back to haunt us in years to come.

Variety is the gift of learning to savor life at every level. We go to the children's baseball games because we love doing it, not because we feel we must do it. We take family time and play time and reading time and rest time because each of them makes us a fuller human being. Then we have new energy to take to our work rather than feeling our work drain energy out of the rest of our lives.

Self-awareness is the monitor of the heart that tells us when we're too tired too often to be able to really enjoy life, to be our best selves for everyone around us. When the fatigue settles into the center of our souls, when we get up as tired as we were when we went to bed, when we only half-listen, half-read, half-smile, and half-care about anything anymore, we are inclining dangerously to one side. It is time to tilt heavily to the other.

Re-creation is the virtue that sends us off to cleanse the palate of our souls from the noxious residues of yesterday. It is that one single activity — the piano or the bowling team, the fishing boat or the woods, the workshop or the computer class — that makes us forget yesterday's concerns and makes us young of soul again.

Imperfection is the gift that saves us from destroying ourselves in the name of some apotheosis of excellence that exists only in our own mind. It is the delusion of perfection that drives us to live so imperfectly. There are some things in life worth doing that are worth doing poorly. When being perfect in one aspect of life destroys the rest of life for us, it is time to lean, lean, lean as far away from it as possible before we stop doing what only we can do in this place, with these people, at this time.

Life without stress can be a very stagnant life. What must we do when enough is enough? For the sake of our very souls, we must lean, lean, lean to the other side.

CHAPTER 14

Does Anything Really Matter?

Sometimes it is very difficult to know what life is actually all about. Ideals fade, and what were once driving personal goals suddenly lose their appeal. But more than that, even the world around us shifts and slants from one commitment to another.

In one period of history the ultimate attainment of the human enterprise purports to be "a chicken in every pot." In another decade, it becomes rugged individualism again. Then people who, for whatever reason, cannot fend for themselves in that kind of environment are left once more to sleep in the parks.

At other times, some people get rich speculating and others get poor working. Universal standards disappear. The whole notion of the common good or social absolutes simply evaporates.

When all is said and done, as our own lives move from stage to stage, from era to era, we get the idea that somewhere along the line someone changed the rules and forgot to tell us.

What they told us in childhood, for instance, the unmitigated imperatives, the bedrocks of an honest life, the hallmarks of a decent society — honesty, hard work, fair play, and kindness — have become, in our own time, the public fodder of the daily press. Members of Congress, even presidents, lie, we discover. Business executives with more money than they can count, let alone spend, cheat the very people who can't afford to lose a penny. The big bombers of powerful nations grind the populations of small countries into ash. People work hard all their lives and then discover that their pensions have been stolen or that their companies have moved to countries not bound to the same labor laws and salary protections as our own. The country passes immigration legislation and then fails to monitor it until we have a whole labor force of low paid, exploited, illegal laborers here, too.

The things that matter, the very constants of life, all of a sudden don't seem to matter at all anymore.

Some people call that lack of commitment to clear norms or goals "freedom." The problem with that attitude is that it's not true. There simply is no such thing as unbounded freedom. No one goes through life borne on the wind of personal whim and whimsy. No one is really absolved of public constraints. We owe order to one another, for the sake of our own personal security on public highways, if nothing else.

Nor is anyone free of personal priorities. Everybody steers by some star. Everybody is bound to something, striving for something, driven by something, intent on getting something, even if it is nothing more than personal pleasure. The only question is, What do we really want? Where does it come from? What is its purpose? And in the end, will it really matter in the grand scale of human endeavors?

At one stage of life, popularity matters. At another stage, approval matters. At a later stage, success — whatever our personal definition of it — matters. At its final stages, at least in the West, physical security matters. But none of them last. Each of them comes and goes, waxes and wanes, becomes more or less important as life goes by. None of them answers the question of what will really count when we look back at it all from the Mount Olympus of our own life.

What is it, if anything, that matters enough to move us from stage to stage? Or, even more important, is there anything that matters to us so much that whatever happens to our social status as a result of it, we will nevertheless survive the loss of it?

If we find ourselves pitted against authority — seeking justice, seeking truth, seeking voice — what can possibly sustain us in so uneven a contest?

When the desire to be popular and to have social approval drives us, we have to ask ourselves whether we control this need for acceptance or whether it controls us. How much would we be willing to do to be popular with those more well-connected than we? How far are we prepared to go to be approved by those more powerful than we? Are there no measures we will not exceed? And if there are, what are they?

If the need to be a success, by whatever standards, is what motivates us, prods us to do more and more and more, what is the more we really seek? Is it really money — or is it prestige? Is it achievement — or is it power? How much more of anything must we possess in order to be satisfied with ourselves? By what internal standards do we measure ourselves?

If security is the ghost within, what will we forego now in order to be sure that we will be safe at some other mythical, uncertain, still distant time in life? Will it be risk or play or friends we give up to fill the coffers of our heart with the assurance that we will be certain of something in the future? In that case, even the essence of humanity, open-hearted and unstinting, stands to curdle in us undeveloped as a result.

No doubt about it. What matters to us matters all our lives. It makes all the difference between real success and ultimate insignificance, between approval and character, between security and selfishness, between popularity and leadership.

What matters to us is, in the long run, no small concern both to our life direction and to our character. Spiritual traditions everywhere deal with the question sooner or later. In Jewish spirituality, the answer to that question is a central one.

The rabbis tell this story:

Once upon a time, Moshe Leib spent seven years in the House of Study of the holy Rabbi of Nikolsburg. When the seven years were up, the rabbi summoned him and said nothing but: "Now you may go home."

Then he gave him three things to take with him: a small coin called a ducat, a loaf of bread, and the kind of long white ceremonial robe called a *khalat*. Finally, he added, "And may the love of Israel enter your heart."

Moshe Leib walked all day and grew very tired. In the evening, as he approached a village where he intended to eat his bread and pass the night, he heard the sound of groaning and found that it came from behind a barred cellar window. He went up to it, spoke to the person inside, and soon learned that it was a Jewish innkeeper who had been imprisoned because he had not been able to pay his rent to the lord of the estate. The first thing Moshe Leib did was to throw his loaf of bread through the bars.

Then, as if it were his own region, he made straight for the manor house, asked to be taken to the lord, and requested him to release the Jew. He offered his ducat as ransom.

The lord of the manor merely looked at this impudent fellow who was attempting to settle a debt of three hundred gulden with a ducat, and sent him packing. But the instant Moshe Leib was outside, he was so overcome with the suffering of the imprisoned Jew that he burst in at the door again and cried: "But you must let him go! Take my ducat and let the man go free!"

Now in those days every lord in the state of Poland was a king on his own estate and had the power of life and death. So the lord ordered his servants to seize Moshe Leib and throw him into the kennel.

Because Moshe Leib saw death in the eyes of the dogs who rushed at him, he quickly put on his white *khalat,* so as to die in a festive robe. But at the sight of the *khalat* the dogs backed toward the wall and howled.

When the lord entered the kennel, Moshe Leib was still leaning close to the door and the dogs were still standing in a wide circle, howling and shivering. The lord took one look at the situation and told him to get out and be off!

But Moshe Leib insisted: "Not until you take my ducat and let the man go free!"

Then the lord took the ducat and himself went to the house where the Jew was imprisoned, opened the cellar door, and bade the man go home in peace.

And Moshe Leib continued his journey.

The Rabbi of Tchortkov, we are told, loved to tell this story. And when he finished he always added: "Oh, where can that kind of *khalat* be found?"

The story is a subtle one. It is, at first sight, only a story about one student of Torah who cared more for the life of others than he did for his own. But it is actually a frozen moment in time meant to be a measuring stick for our own spiritual growth.

Moshe Leib, we are tempted to think, is protected for some strange reason by his outward appearance. But that is impossible. The garment, a ceremonial robe given in memory of his years of Torah study, does nothing but mark what he should be as a student of God's word, not necessarily what he really is. What could be more obvious? The robe is not magic; the robe is simply a robe. No, what protects Moshe Leib, in the end, is not the ceremonial robe. It is precisely what is under his ceremonial robe — his own commitment to life, to justice, to the law above the law, and to an authority beyond any authorities who use their power for their own aggrandizement rather than for the good of others.

The Rabbi of Tchortkov loves the story because it unmasks all the public pretense such honors so often engender. "Oh, where can that kind of *khalat* be found?" he cries as he pokes fun at those who would even dare to think that it was the robe — the public trappings, the appearance — of Moshe Leib that saved him. That kind of robe, the old rabbi knows, can be found only in the heart of the person who wears it.

What drives Moshe Leib, what protects him from death of soul and discouragement of spirit, is not the robe he wears but what the ceremonial robe is meant to signal. It is the sign of what has formed him. It is the evidence of what is in him: the Jewish commitment to Torah — his seven years in the House of Study — the reflexive acts of loving kindness he shows with the sacrifice of his own food and money to a starving man — and his commitment to the lord of heaven rather than the lord of the manor. Those are the compass points that guide Moshe Leib through a difficult part of his life "as if it were his own region."

These are the things that really matter to Moshe Leib. This is what, in the end, saves him. His love of Israel — its tradition and law — and everything it stands for means more to him than all the success, all the security, all the approval, and all the personal popularity his little world has to offer.

We are left to wonder, then, what really matters to us. If what matters to us most is being in sync with the world around us, we stand to corrupt our hearts with the yearnings of others rather than the wisdom of our own. The distinction is important. The story reminds us that what we form our hearts on, what we do because of what we say we are, is the only thing that can possibly make our footsteps sure when the darkness comes, as dark always does to every life.

If the question is, then, Does anything really matter? the answer must surely be that only those things matter for which we would risk our own public approval, our own security, our personal popularity, and even our eventual success. Everything else is either mere show or empty-heartedness, the kind that is, at best, only a shallow impersonation of the fullness of humanity toward which we all strive.

CHAPTER 15

Why Was I Born?

I remember the first time I saw her. I've been thinking about it ever since.

I remember the shock of it. The tragedy of it. The futility of it. The downright embarrassing implications of it.

Should I look at her — or not look at her?

Should I kneel down to talk to her — or just keep standing there, in the fullness of my health, while she struggled to get her wheelchair into a position that would make eye contact possible for both of us?

Should I do her a favor and simply tell her she wasn't fit for the situation, no matter how much it hurt, no matter how hard it would be to say it?

Should I send her away immediately — or let her stay just long enough to find out for herself that she could not possibly function in this setting?

I'd passed people on the street who were also handicapped, also "physically challenged," as they called it now, also confined to wheelchairs. Often. But, in those cases, I hadn't had to look at them or talk to them about their futures or meet the question straight on. "I want to be part of this," Mary Louise said. "I'm sure I'm supposed to be here."

I knew what a wheelchair was like. After all, I'd been in one myself for almost two years. But wheelchairs were for getting out of — and she was never going to get out of this one again. In fact, she had been living in this chair since she was four years old. She couldn't stand, couldn't sit up straight on her own without a steel body brace, couldn't move more than the thumb with which she operated the chair, couldn't turn her head.

What kind of a life could she possibly have here, I wondered?

But by the time Mary Louise died, she had taught us all a thing or two about life. She went for "walks" outside in her chair regularly because she "needed to smell the grass," she said. She couldn't stand being cooped up. Getting out "was healthy for you," she figured.

She loved to "dance" and whirled her wheelchair around and around the floor as the music played. "I'll dance in heaven," she said, "so I have to start here."

She went to movies and out to dinner with friends. She wrote letters on the Voice Recognition Program on her computer all day long to people from one end of the country to the other. She had company come to see her constantly.

She did regular spiritual direction with people who thought they had problems till they walked into the room and saw her.

She had a degree in English literature and loved to work on the liturgy planning team.

She liked to travel and took regular vacations.

She moved into an Independent Living Home for a year or so because she wanted to make sure that she had had the experience of living alone.

After a while it got difficult to remember the wheelchair when you talked to her.

When Mary Louise died, the chapel was packed with the people she'd helped through life — friends, clients, directees — and full, too, of the people who had helped her through life but who, over the years, found it difficult to remember the wheelchair.

She had lived all her life with people feeding her, bathing her, bedding her, and dressing her. But she died fully alive.

I can't help but think of all the people I've met who had either been imprisoned by circumstances and allowed that imprisonment to stop their growth or who had imprisoned themselves in their fears or their passions and refused to grow beyond them.

Life, I came to realize — thanks to this woman who could never for a moment take it for granted — is a choice.

But choosing is not easy. There are so many things to choose from, after all. We can choose to spend our lives chasing physical fitness — trying to look 25 when we're 60. Or we can give ourselves to storing up money far beyond what it takes to live a decent life. Maybe what we are intent on gathering is power in excess of our abilities to sustain it. Maybe it is simply a need to the point of uselessness for whatever happens to be today's equivalent of "bread and circuses," the old Roman designation of "the good life," the abandonment to hedonism.

Indeed, it is the choices we make as we go that, before it's over, stand to break our heart. When we make a life out of things not worth a life, then we live with a sagging sense of futility. "What's it all about?" becomes the most depressing question of them all. It's a sure sign that we are waiting for the answers to life to come from outside ourselves when, in fact, the real answer to the value of life can come only from inside ourselves.

Down deep inside ourselves lie both our highest aspirations and our most frustrated hopes, the brambles of life that scar our souls and distort our vision of the present. They lead us to doubt what is doable, even what is desirable. They tell us that what we are is not enough to deal with what is needed in life.

And oh, we give ourselves so many reasons to excuse ourselves from the excitement of being alive. We can't do some things because we're too slow, we say. We can't do other things because we're too weak. We can't do many things because we're too unprepared. We can't do other things because we're not fully equipped for them. We can't do much because we don't have the power or the position or the social connections or the money. And so we do nothing. And so we go through life mourning what we do not have and grieving what we have not tried to do.

But to deny our aspirations, to pronounce impossible what we have yet to try, is the beginning of the end. It is the beginning of the end of world peace. It is the beginning of the end of a loving relationship. It is the beginning of the end of what is meant to be a truly valuable, a truly happy life.

Being born is not about choice, true, but living life well is. The choices we make as life goes on — not where, when, or how we are born — determine the quality of the life we live. It is what we do with what we have, not our social status or our physical endowments, that will make the difference in the end between what we are and what we make of it.

Every spiritual tradition on earth concentrates on identifying the criteria by which a human being lives not only the most ethical, not only the most moral of human lives, but the most holy as well. Jewish spirituality is clear about the relationship between being one thing, good enough in itself, and becoming another that is even better, even more of what we all say we are, whatever the circumstances of our lives. The rabbis tell this story:

> Once upon a time, a congregation became very concerned because their old rabbi had taken to disappearing from the synagogue after the opening of Shabbat. Some were afraid he was forgetting his proper duties. Some worried that he was actually breaking the Sabbath laws. Some, knowing his reputation for holiness, insisted that he must be being spirited up to heaven, perhaps even by Elijah himself, to discuss holy questions, to escape the problems of the age.
>
> So to settle the concerns among them, one Sabbath night they dispatched a spy to follow him and report where he was going.
>
> Sure enough, no sooner had the Sabbath candles been lit than the old man slipped out of the synagogue, walked quietly down the path, through the woods, and up a tall mountain. Finally, following quietly behind, the spy could see a small cabin in the distance. And sure enough, the rabbi went straight toward it. The spy crept closer. A few more steps and the spy could see the rabbi framed in the doorway by the soft light of a dying fire.
>
> The spy slipped around to the side of the cabin and pressed his face to the window. He could never have imagined the scene he saw. There on a cot lay an old gentile woman, her face sallow, her breathing slow.
>
> First, the rabbi swept the floor. Then the rabbi chopped new wood and fed the fire. Next the rabbi drew clean water from the well. Finally, the rabbi made a cauldron of fresh soup and set it on the bedstand by her side.
>
> The spy sped back down the mountain and through the woods to make his report: "Well," the congregation said, some with disdain, some with hope, "did our rabbi go up to heaven?"

The spy stopped for a moment to think. "No," the spy said. "The rabbi did not go up to heaven. The rabbi went much higher than that."

In every instance, each tradition defines holiness as that which transcends what is normally expected of us in order to achieve what is fully human and, therefore, breathtakingly holy. In one sense, holiness is that dimension of us which simply surpasses what can rightly be expected of the average human being in order to become, in another sense, everything that can possibly be expected of a human being who is fully human.

There are many obstacles to physical development, of course. There are no obstacles to human development whatsoever.

If the question, on bad days, on days when I doubt the purpose of life, on days when I am unsatisfied with the life I am living, is, Why was I ever born? the answer seems to be a simple one: we are born to finish what God has left undone.

Moshe Leib put it this way: "If someone comes to you and asks your help, you shall not turn him off with pious words, saying: 'Have faith and take your troubles to God!' You shall act as if there were no God, as if there were only one person in all the world who could help this person — only yourself."

Mary Louise could not be expected to do anything in the physical sense of the word. And she didn't. There might even be those who, seeing her, would wonder how such a life could possibly be fulfilled. But it is exactly what she did despite the fact that she could do nothing that made her life the enspirited force it was to the rest of us. Clearly, we would all have been a great deal worse off if she had not been born.

CHRISTIAN LOVE

CHAPTER 16

Why Can't I Just Get Away from It All?

"I just want to get away from it all," people report so casually these days. It's become a modern mantra. "We're going to get away from it all," people say when they go on vacation. "I need to get away from it all," we tell ourselves when our nerves begin to tighten and the tone of voice changes from welcoming to terse. "There's just no way to get away from it all," we say of the office and the house and the family and the deadlines and the phone and the schedule. And it's true. In the Far East, silence gives space. In the West, there is no silence and no space either. The streets are alive with bellowing and boom boxes, calling and whistling, the belch of busses and the screech of tires. Where is the space for soul in all of this?

And I ought to know. I'm one of the people on the globe who are looking for it. In fact, if truth were known, I'm one of the people who regularly takes off in pursuit of it. Even monasteries, in an era of planes, trains, and automobiles, are not safe from the feeling of bustle that comes with the steady string of meetings and projects, phone calls and guests that every monastery hosts.

So, each year, I get away from it all to write. I go alone to a tiny stone cottage overlooking Derrynane Bay in the west of Ireland and watch the fog roll in and the waves roll in and the rain roll in and the mist roll out. Day after day after day. It takes about a week before I can feel my heart slow down enough to hear the words come out of the center of me.

No doubt about it: getting away from it all is part of the culture now. In a world where people jostle one another on elevators and in doorways and store aisles and street corners and shopping malls and traffic every day of our lives, getting away is part of the process of becoming human again.

But that kind of getting away is temporary. Here, where I am on the mountainside, it's permanent. The houses on the hill are blocks apart. People don't see one another from one week to the next. Only the pubs and the churches promise any kind of regular contact with the rest of the human race in a place where the shepherds spend all day following the sheep and the women spend most of the day cooking for the shepherds. So are things any better here?

Of course they are. At least in some ways.

Getting away from it all, finding the comfort of empty quiet and familiar routine, puts us back in touch with ourselves. The fracturing of the self stops for a while. You find that you are where you are for a change instead of being in one place but thinking about another. Here you don't worry about where you're going tomorrow because it's very unlikely that you're going anywhere at all. There is nowhere else to go and little way to get there even if there were. So the pace of life slows to a trickle. Nobody just "drops in." Social life becomes an event, not a routine: you don't see people you don't invite in. Then, when they come, you make an event of it. Dinner parties here go on for hours. First, you have supper at one house; then, some weeks later, those same people come to yours. Sometimes you meet in the pub to watch a national sporting event on a fourteen-inch television set propped up on a bracket in a corner. There are no booths. The village simply stands there, heads crooked back, and watches together while everyone waits for someone new to walk in. "Good craic," the Irish call it, and they mean "good fun," finally, to be with someone other than the self.

But there is another side to that kind of world as well. Clearly it is as easy to feel stagnant in a place like this as it is to feel jangled in a place like a city.

Which of these conditions is the most spiritual, then? Which of them is most likely to keep us balanced, make us whole, give us spirit, raise our energies, till our souls? Answer: only both.

The history of religion is a veritable who's who of people who are apparently dedicated to "getting away from it all." Monks of every ilk — swamis and spiritual gurus, nuns and Sufis, rabbis and hermits — all spend time "away" in silence or in physical retreat from the ordinary routines of the world around them. But they never stay there. Why? These are the people who really can "just quit and get away from it all." So why don't they?

The honest answer is a simple one: for the Christian, life is made for the living of it, not for hiding from it. It is a life spent "following the Jesus" who walked from Galilee to Jerusalem, healing lepers, giving sight to the blind, raising people from the dead, contesting with the leaders of both the temple and the empire.

Not surprisingly, then, the Rule of Benedict, that ancient spiritual document dedicated to enfleshing the following of Jesus for monastics in the Western world, is very direct about the answer to the question. Hermits, common to the period in which Benedict of Nursia began his monasteries in the early sixth century, were respected but not considered the norm of religious life. One translation of the Rule puts it this way: "The second kind of monks are the anchorites; that is, the hermits — those who, not by the new fervour of a conversion but by the long probation of life in a monastery, have learned to fight against the devil, having already been taught by the solace of many. They, having been well prepared in the army of brothers for the solitary fight of the hermit, being secure now without the consolation of another, are able, God helping them, to fight with their own hand or arm against the vices of the flesh or of their thoughts." No romanticism here.

The point is clear: to be a hermit is fine, the Benedictine is taught, but not forever, and not only. The solitary life, Benedict says, is only for those who have already been trained, "by the long probation of life in a monastery," to control themselves in the hurly-burly of society that the rest of us are trying to avoid.

Benedict of Nursia was not the only spiritual master of his time, therefore, to warn against confusing the desire for escape with the desire for a spiritual life. In fact, a story is told of Abbot Anthony the Great himself, the first famous hermit of Western monasticism, who had spent his entire life as either hermit or community abbot, which teaches us a great deal about the spiritual as well as the human dimensions of the spiritual life.

Once upon a time, Abba Anthony went to visit Abba Amoun in Mount Nitria. When they met, Abba Amoun said, "By your prayers, the number of the brethren increases. Now some of them want to build more cells where they may live in peace. How far away from here do you think we should build those cells?"

Abba Anthony said, "Well, first, let us eat at the ninth hour. Then, when we have eaten, let us go out for a walk in the desert and explore the country."

So they went out into the desert and they walked until sunset. Then Abba Anthony said, "Let us pray and plant the cross here so that those who wish to do so may build here. Then when those who remain there want to visit those who have come here, they can take a little food at the ninth hour and then come.

"If they do this, they will be able to keep in touch with each other without distraction of mind."

The distance from the first monastery to the second is twelve miles.

The story brings a smile to the face of any honest monastic. Here we have two abbots, renowned for their sanctity, clothed in mystique, known for their asceticism, quibbling about where to put a monastery full of her-mits. Answer: as far away as possible from any other living human being, of course. Except that they don't. They put it in a place where the monas-tics — hermits, remember — would be able to visit one another daily if they wanted. But why? And what does their decision about the proximity of one monastery to another have to say to the rest of humankind about life and holiness, growth and human development?

Indeed, the story is a telling one. It dampens the romanticism that of-ten undergirds the desire to "get away from it all." It exposes us to our-selves.

The fact is that, however pressured we feel, however intent on distanc-ing ourselves from the stressors in our life, isolation is not the answer.

Abbot Anthony, hermit and monk, knew the ways of the human heart. He knew that eventually, once the pressure lifts, we will move like magnets to the opposite pole, to the other side of ourselves, to the part of us that is partial and in search of those others who make us whole.

The real spiritual lesson in the story is that we need one another — all of us. Whatever we lack, the others supply. Whatever they are looking for is more than likely, at least in part, in us.

This new monastery, the one being founded by the very monks who "want to live in peace," Anthony suggests, should be only twelve miles from the first, just a half day's walk away from the parent community. Near enough to get back to when going back is the only hope we have of finding our way forward.

On the other hand, the time will come, Anthony knows, when "living in peace" will not be the answer. Then only living in community will be able to make up for the void in us. Then it will be the guidance, the support, the spirit of the other that pulls us through.

It comes down to the fact, in the long run, that we are not meant, in most cases, to lead separated lives. We need, as these two third-century abbots did, the possibility of morning breaks together.

We require, natural solitaries or not, the opportunity at times to take a companionable stroll through the deserts of our lives with others who walk the same path, in the hope that they can see the terrain for us with fresh eyes.

We need to reflect with others on the questions that plague us. We seek to discern with others who may be more wise than ourselves. We crave to know the opinions of those less involved than ourselves in the issues that face us, for fear our very proximity to them blinds us as much as it commits us.

We need to give our own gifts of self, as well, so that we ourselves do not become the shrine of the very small god at which we adore.

Why don't we just leave where we are, quit what we're doing and "get away from it all"? Because we can't. Because it simply isn't possible. First, the power of the familiar itself will forever call us back. Where we come from is a large part of who we are. It is the root of our identity, the place of our growing. It cannot simply be put down because it is not outside of us; it is inside of us — and always will be. Wrestling with the roots of us is part of human spiritual growth.

Can we step out into the dark alone every once in a while — just to taste new air and forget for a while the old impossibles? Indeed. We can and we must, if for no other reason than to get the perspective on them that distance provides. But can we ever really put them down? No. As Tennyson writes in "Ulysses," we are "part of all that we have met." There is no being our real selves without them.

Second, more than the natural attraction to the familiar, though, is the obvious awareness that there is a need in all of us to go forward, to go beyond ourselves. The desire for new direction, then, always calls us forward. It isn't long before, alone, we empty ourselves of our own wisdom and need to fill it up again somehow. Then we need to look outside of ourselves for the insights of others. We realize that we must compare our own experiences to the awarenesses of those who have gone down the road before us, both to set our course and to measure our steps.

Finally, we do not live for our own sakes. Like the Magi of the Christmas story, we all come bearing gifts of gold, frankincense, and myrrh — resources, spirit, and healing — that are given to us for the sake of others so that the world may become a better place because we have been here. After all, we follow the Jesus who gave all his gifts away for the sake of those others to come.

"Getting away from it all," then, is a myth. That is not the purpose of life. The purpose of life is to go where we need to go — wherever that is — in order to get more of what our souls must have in order to pour ourselves out again.

CHAPTER 17

What Does It Take to
Put Excitement Back into Life?

I don't really know the woman whose letter echoed with such intensity through so much of the rest of my correspondence. If she walked into this room right now, I would not recognize her. But actually, that's not exactly true. It is, in fact, a very superficial attempt to depersonalize a very universal reality. The truth is that I do know her — very well — and so do you. If she's not "everywoman," she is certainly "almost everywoman." Better yet, she's anyone, woman or man, who has spent her life grinding out one day after another, ideals high, burdens heavy, life routine.

When her letter came, I knew that I was listening to the life truth of more people than most of us would care to admit — even ourselves at times.

She wrote: "I am a 55-year-old woman and was introduced to your writings about 10 years ago. But at that time I was a single mother trying to raise children. I was only concerned with and would only allow myself the possibility of buying books as gifts for children. I gave as a gift your book, *A Passion for Life.*"

I stopped and thought a minute. Here was a young middle-aged woman who, for whatever reason, found herself alone in midlife, no financial support, no companion — and no choice. There were children to raise, bills to pay. And so she got on with it: she bought little for herself, she balanced home and work, she concentrated on the children — their needs, their schedules, their formation. She bought them books, not trinkets or gadgets or exotic trips to strange places in the style of those who can afford to live life at another level.

She had no time and little money to spend on herself. Life was simply a matter of living it, of going on, of doing what must be done, of doing what you never imagined you would be doing — and of doing it day after day, year after year. She was happy, of course, in that quiet sense of the word that means more "not unhappy" than "excited by life." If truth were known, she was maybe more numbed by life than even challenged by it.

Whatever had brought her to this point in life lived now more in memory than in fact — if it still lived in her at all, that is. By this time, surely, whatever had created this situation for her in her life had long ago lost the power of raw pain and simply settled into some kind of half-conscious ache.

Then, as I read on, I realized that there had been a shift in the letter, almost imperceptible but audible, nevertheless. As I listened to the words under the words, felt the pace of them quicken, heard the slightly rising crescendo in the tone of them, I began to sense some light as well as darkness in it. The letter went on, "Now the children are grown and I have returned to school. I am enrolled in an MA program in Culture and Spirituality and I hope to go on to a doctoral program."

I smiled a bit. Here was a woman who had not only come through a time of total suppression of the self and begun to live again; this was also a woman who intended, now that she had been able to begin again, to keep on going. She was 55, and she had her eyes on the summit. She was going straight uphill — no looking back — and, furthermore, she intended to go all the way. No whining about what some might call a late start, no apologia for what she could not do, no intention whatsoever to settle for less than wild possibility, total spiritual insurrection. She would be new beyond all predictions, above any and all measurements, in excess of any of the standard predictions for women who were single mothers in their mid-50s.

The point is that it was not lost time she was counting; it was not social custom she courted. It was what the philosophers loved to call the "élan vital," the zeal to be. It was experience she wanted. It was beingness she sought. It was the eternal sparkle of the soul she intended to rekindle.

I put the letter down on the desk for a minute and looked out the window. It is not often that we get the chance to watch a resurrection in progress, but it is always a blessing. Watching someone else come to life again, being able to feel the pulse beat in a letter from someone across the country whom you have never met but whose life you recognize so easily, brings new life to your own. Here, you find yourself saying to yourself, is hope at the flash point, a sign of things to come, a symbol of what must be. This is the story of life refusing to die.

This is a woman who has indeed "put excitement back into life" and challenges the rest of us to do the same.

"The purpose of my letter," she went on, "is to thank you for . . . your stalwart position on the right of each of us to find our own story."

When I finished the letter, I knew that there was a serious difference between insisting on the right of people to find their own story and the willingness, the courage, the determination of those people to do it. I'd like to think that I had something to do with encouraging a woman to begin again, of course. But it is the mettle of the woman herself that made the difference. Life, the letter signaled clearly, is a choice. Not always, perhaps. We are all thrown into so many things not of our own making, not of our own desire. But ultimately, it is what's inside of us, not what's outside of us that makes the difference.

Everyone gets into periods in their lives that seem endlessly grey, totally gone. Life always ends before it begins again, just as night precedes day. That is exactly what spiritual resurrection is all about. It is also what psychological resurrection implies.

To be really alive we must be willing to put down one phase of life after another, to refuse to spend life treading water in any one phase. Life is for the living, for those who intend to keep on living, whatever the cost, because to do anything else is to betray creation.

The monastics of the desert, the very people who might be most easily accused of sacrificing life for a living death, may have understood better than most the place of excitement in life if a soul is to live in the flush of it, be filled to the edges with it, sanctify all of it.

It was said of Abba Agathon that he spent a long time building a cell with his disciples. At last, when it was finished, they came to live there.

But Agathon saw something about the place during the first days of it that seemed harmful. So he said to his disciples, "Get up, let us leave this place."

They were dismayed and said to him, "If you had already decided to move, why have we taken so much trouble building the cell? People will be scandalized at us and will say, 'Look at them, moving again; what unstable people!'"

He saw that they were held back by timidity so he said to them, "If some are scandalized, others, on the contrary, will be much edified and will say, 'How blessed are they who go away for God's sake, having no other care.'"

And then he added, "However, let him who wants to come, come; as for me, I am going."

Then they understood and prostrated themselves to the ground and begged him to allow them to go with him.

We should all be so lucky as to have a model in our lives of someone who is not afraid to move on when things are not right in life. When all the obligations have been met, but all the boundaries of life have not been explored in the doing of them, all the dimensions of life have not been ripened by them, it is time to go.

Abba Agathon knew that simply the building of the cell was itself enough. He had gotten everything in life out of it that the cell could possibly give him, and he knew it. He had done what needed to be done to complete that part of life. Now, if he wanted to go on growing, there was nothing to do but to leave it.

He saw something about the cell itself, whatever it was, that told him that the cell was now more obstacle than challenge to his spiritual development, more weight than spring to his soul. He knew that life takes growing into if we are ever really to come home to ourselves. He had come to realize that settling down satisfied with what is, with what we've achieved so far, what we've garnered, what we've secured for ourselves — even spiritually — can be the worst thing that can happen to a soul.

The disciples, on the other hand, operated on principles that bind most of us more than we like to think: What will people think? they wondered. Will they call us moody, flighty, unstable? Or now, here, this time in my life, will they call me foolish, maybe, or a scandal, maybe, or unstable, maybe? In a midlife crisis, perhaps? Or worse, all of the above? Probably. Some will. But there will be just as many others who, seeing us reach for the stars, will begin another race, start to build a new part of life themselves, as a result. "They," as Agathon knows, "will be edified," will say to themselves, "If she can do it, so can I. If he can risk it, so can I. If they are willing to begin again, why not I?"

Excitement seldom comes unbidden to a life. If we want to put excitement back into our lives, we must be willing to put it there ourselves. We must be willing to change directions when the path we're on has become more a cul-de-sac that leads only back to where we once began than a path that moves us forward in life.

Sometimes the changes are simple ones — like learning to garden very late in life — but they are never without purpose. I begin something to learn something new. I join things to get out of the house for a change or to meet new people or to exercise or simply to stop doing nothing but the same old things. I join to give my soul an airing.

Sometimes the changes are momentous — like marrying again or going back to school or changing jobs.

Sometimes the changes are meant not so much to change my life as to stir my soul. I begin to read a book a little every day. I begin to take weekends away alone. I begin to see a spiritual director. I begin to take photography lessons. I join a beginner's bowling team on Tuesday nights.

But whatever the reason, whatever the purpose of the activity itself, I know deep down that, for the first time in a long time, I have added a touch of spice to the bland that is my life. My mind wakes up; my heart starts to smile a bit; my soul gets dusted off and begins to shine again.

It is so easy to die before we have ever begun to live. Having spent life doing all the things a person is expected to do — finish school, decide on a profession, get a job, make a living, find a house, settle down — someday I discover, if I'm lucky, that I've seldom done anything out of time or just because I wanted to do it or because I refused to live another thirty years doing what I've been doing for the last thirty.

The insight is electric: I am alive, finally alive!

If the question is, What does it take to put excitement back into life? the answer is a simple one. It takes me doing something I've never done. It takes the willingness in me to move beyond my lifelong boundaries, out of my comfort zone, into the void. It may even require me to do it alone, if necessary, but always with a purpose.

Agathon said it so clearly: "Let him who wants to come, come; as for me, I am going."

Now, isn't that exciting?

Chapter 18

How Will I Know Truth When I See It?

Monasteries are curious places. To the occasional monastery-watcher, they can seem so uniform, so boringly organized. Monastics, for the most part, live a common schedule, say a common set of prayers, live under a common Rule of life. They eat together, live together, work together day after day for years and are formed together all their lives. The inclination is to assume that monastic communities are one-dimensional places that spawn one-dimensional people. Maybe, but not in any monastery I know, regardless of the tradition, however undifferentiated the group. Not in my monastery for sure.

In fact, I sat with a group of Eastern and Western monastics at an international meeting recently, fascinated by their apparent sameness and acutely aware of the differences among them at the same time. They all wore long robes. (But no, come to think about it, they didn't. I didn't, for instance.) They all wore some identifying mark, at least — beads or pins, or crosses, or colors of robes or shawls or cinctures.

The swamis came in wearing orange robes but soon began to appear in small wool skull caps — a grey one here, a white one there. The Buddhists wore sandals, some with socks, some without them. The Western monastics wore robes or pants, simple street clothes or long burka-like dresses.

All of them, almost every one of them, in other words, deviated at least a bit from the norms of even their own groups. Who was the perfect monastic, then? Who was the one who lived the monastic ideal most truly? And did it matter? Did it really affect the degree to which they lived the real monastic ideal? What was truth here, where, even among those most intent on putting down all the nonessentials of life, no absolute norm seemed to apply?

Then, all of a sudden, I began to wonder if the real question might now be, Is uniformity really a measure of anything, including holiness? Maybe it is we who have the great need to reduce sanctity to some kind of spiritual sameness. Maybe those who are truly simple and open to the workings of God in life are the ones who know best that it is very easy to make a god even out of devotion, even out of detachment, even out of self-effacement. Is it really self-effacing to have to stand out for being perfectly self-effacing?

I have often wondered over the years whether it isn't precisely what appears to be a common mold that is itself the ground for differences. Isn't difference in the face of the commonplace the very sign of the singular and intimate relationship between God and every one of us, individual and separate? Here in the place of homogeneity, in fact, the most minuscule differences glare like beacons in the night.

However uniform monastics may look, differences mark us like the mist of soft snow in winter, barely visible and silent — but certain. So, in all our sameness, differences abound.

If anything, then, monasteries are a study, a reminder to us all, of the irrepressible in human nature. Behind every long leather cincture or plain black belt lives a personality that, like the rest of us, is struggling its perfectly particular way toward God. At least ours did.

Sister Rosalia, for instance, had been a first-grade teacher all her life. Her soul operated on an invisible clock. She walked out the door of the small convent in which we lived to cross the church parking lot to her classroom at the same time every morning, and she returned at the same time every night. Rosalia was the epitome of regularity, and order, and fidelity.

She was what my novice mistress called a model of the "living Rule." She kept silence — always at night, almost always during the day. She never consorted with "seculars." She walked head down, eyes on the ground — just as the spiritual masters for centuries had recommended we do as an aid to acquiring perpetual "recollection" or consciousness of God. Her room was sparse and antiseptic to the core. She cut no corners, took no liberties, strayed from none of the disciplines.

Sister Rosalia was the walking symbol of the ideal. Somebody's ideal, at least.

Sister Marie Claire, on the other hand, was not.

Sister Marie Claire, a music teacher, lived strewing beauty wherever she went. She had mysterious ways of getting cut flowers of extraordinary color for her music room, grew pots full of African violets large and full and in jungle proportions everywhere. They covered every window sill in her music room, overflowed into the guest parlors, grew recklessly in the solarium, multiplied and multiplied and multiplied. Marie Claire brought a sense of abundance to life.

As far as Marie Claire was concerned, nothing was impossible, nothing was forbidden. People flocked to her music room for counsel, for support, for fun. She stayed there — long after the little music students had gone home, long after the rest of us had already gone upstairs to read in silence — meeting people, holding court. You could hear the laughter, muted but regular, wafting up the front stairwell far into the evening hours.

Marie Claire lived, generous and open-hearted, an Auntie Mame figure who swept into every room with a smile on her face and a warm handshake or arm hold for every person there.

Marie Claire was no "walking symbol of an otherworldly ideal." No, she was instead an icon of the spirit of religious life, the irrepressible joy that comes with confidence that whatever is, is good — or will be, somehow, someday, somewhere.

Now, here's the problem: Which of them was really true to Truth? Which of them was truly religious? Which of them made religious life true?

The struggle to recognize the truer truth is not new to monasticism or to life in general. Strands of the problem emerge in the definition of sainthood from one century to the next. In almost every case, great people have been identified by some as saints and by others, good people themselves, just as certainly, as sinners. Francis of Assisi, Theresa of Avila, Thomas Merton, Mother Teresa of Calcutta, Pope John XXIII — Jesus — were all a sign of truth to some, a sign of contradiction to others. So how do we know where truth lies?

The monastics of the desert faced the problem, too. They preserved in the monastic literature of the third century a small story that invites us all to go on wrestling with the problem, even here, even now.

Once upon a time, a brother wanted to see Abba Arsenius at Scetis. When he came to the church, he asked the clergy if he could visit with Abba Arsenius.

They said to him, "Brother, have a little refreshment and then go and see him."

But the brother said, "I shall not eat anything till I have met him."

So, because Arsenius's cell was far away, they sent a brother with him. Having knocked on the door, they entered, greeted the old man, and sat down without saying anything. Then the brother from the church said, "I will leave you now. Pray for me."

But the visiting brother, not feeling at ease with the old man, said, "I will come with you," so they both left together.

Then, when they were outside the cell of Abba Arsenius, the visitor said, "Take me to Abba Moses, who used to be a robber."

When they arrived, the Abba welcomed them joyfully. Then, after visiting a while, Abba Moses took leave of them with delight.

The brother who had brought the visitor said to his companion, "See, I have taken you to the foreigner, Arsenius from Rome, and to the Egyptian, Moses. Which of the two do you prefer?"

"As for me," the visitor replied, "I prefer the Egyptian."

Now a Father who heard this prayed to God saying, "Lord, explain this matter to me: for Thy name's sake, the one flees from men, and the other, for Thy name's sake, receives them with open arms."

Now just then two large boats were shown to him on a river, and he saw Abba Arsenius and the Spirit of God sailing in the one, in perfect peace. And in the other was Abba Moses with the angels of God. And they were all eating honey cakes.

We are left with an important question for our own lives: Which of them, Abba Arsenius or Abba Moses, embodied Absolute Truth? And if both did, is Absolute Truth nearly as absolute as we like to think it is? Is the illusion of alternatives really the most untrue thing of all?

Isn't the real truth that both men showed us not only a different spiritual gift but also a different face of the God who is all being, all Truth, as well? In them the truth we really see is that the God of mystery is many-sided. There is no one truth that is the total truth of God. We each embody a bit of it; we all lack the rest of it. Even together we are not the voice of God because we simply do not speak the language or understand the language or know the whole of the language that is the Word of God.

We pretend we do, of course. We tell ourselves and everyone else that we know truth, that we are it, that to be true everyone else must follow us. Such arrogance would be sinful if it weren't so laughable.

And yet we all know, too, that there are some things that are really not true, cannot be true, will never be true.

So what is the key to the recognition of truth? Easy: truth is what truth does. When that which purports to be true — the perfect government, the true church — sins against the truth that must be God, sins against the justice, the goodness, the love, the openness that must be God, then something is untrue about the truth it is teaching.

I was young when I lived with Sister Rosalia and Sister Marie Claire, but I understood the problem immediately. I had to figure out what truth was here. Which one of them really incarnated what it was to be a "religious"? Which one of them was truly a nun? Which one of them gave me the whole picture of what religious life was meant to be?

It took some years to really understand the implications of the question, but eventually I saw what was there for me to see. The truth is that they both, each in her own way, were the best we had to offer.

When Sister Rosalia died — valiant, steady, just a little woman — we cried. The community had lost a saint.

When Sister Marie Claire died — open, great-hearted, free, loving — we cried. The community had lost a saint.

The real truth is that God is too great to be lost in the smallness of any single sliver of life. Truth is One, yes, but truth is many at the same time.

The greatest danger of them all may be in buying into too small a part of the truth. When that happens, change, growth, repentance, and development are impossible. We find ourselves frozen into the shards of yesterday.

If the question is, How shall I know the truth when I see it? the answer must be, truth is that which does the good of God and does it kindly so that none of the people of God are hurt by it.

Truth is the Jesus who said, in the face of the rules, "Rise and walk," and in the face of destructive license, "Go and sin no more," and in the face of irresponsible affluence, "Go and sell what you have and give to the poor," and in the face of human needs, "The Sabbath was made for us, not we for the Sabbath." There are no rules of any institution anywhere that supersede the truth that is the love of God.

Truth is not any one truth, not any one institution, not any one way. Nor can we truly bend ourselves to all of them. Instead, each of us must live out our own singular piece of the truth with love. What else can possibly be the final test of what is truly true?

CHAPTER 19

What's Wrong with Me: Why Can't I Change?

He was my uncle, but frankly, as far as I can remember, unlike all the other in-laws and out-laws, as my dad liked to call them, I saw him only twice in my life. He lived out of state, and people didn't travel much then. I knew a lot about him, nevertheless. I had heard others refer to him for years, but always in hushed tones by the women and short, off-hand remarks and a nod of the head by the men.

It took a while, but I finally got it figured out. This uncle was the kind of son Irish mothers whispered about. He drank. In fact, that's about all he did.

The more you knew about him, I began to notice, the more you turned your face away when his name came up, either in embarrassment for his birth family or out of respect for his new family. Everyone liked his wife or, at the very least, felt sorry for her. She was one of the valiant, they all seemed to agree. There had been one pregnancy after another, I heard the women lament. With every new child, every other child in the family got poorer and poorer and she with them.

I could hear the disgust in the women's voices. There was no talk of alcoholism as a disease, as a sickness, then. These were the days when there was no concept whatsoever of tolerance levels or genetic predispositions to allergenic substances. This was the period of moralizing and disdain and the moral superiority of teetotaling. This was the era of drunken husbands and pregnant women and little or no help for either.

The children of the family, as far as I know, were all basically quiet, even retiring, whatever their own struggles with the situation. I had never heard any hints about fighting or stealing, running away or quitting school. On the contrary, they seemed unusually close — both to their mother and to one another. The oldest boy, barely older than the whole lot of the others, seemed to play father to all of them. And they listened to him. It was a little like watching small children dramatize an adult story.

I remember being taken to visit them. I was an only child and about 12 years old at the time. The thought of getting to know a whole family full of new cousins was the highlight of the summer. I can see them in my mind's eye to this day, all of them dirty and haunted looking, the aunt toothless, the uncle swaggering. I still have a picture of them in my photograph album, lined up on the street in order of birth but each of them otherwise strikingly undistinguished. Their clothes were limp and grey, their hair too long and straggly, their shoes down at the heel. Not one of them stood out. There was simply no energy in the picture at all, none of them mugging, none of them laughing. They just stood there, mute victims of a dust-bowl kind of existence they could do nothing about.

I had never seen anything like it anywhere else in the family. Other uncles drank, after all, but they owned decent homes and sent their children to good schools. Their wives and children wore fresh-pressed clothes and new coats and came to family get-togethers in shiny cars. "What could possibly have gone wrong here?" I asked my mother.

"There is a difference between taking a drink and 'drinking,' Joan," my mother said.

The meaning was clear: This uncle "drank." And that, I came to understand, was a synonym for "did not go to work, did not pay bills, and would not quit drinking." Oh, he quit, the family said — over and over again. It was one good intention after another. For a while, the family would thrive. But it never lasted. In the end, he always went back to the bar. Always. It went on like that for years. He would be drunk for weeks, then sober for a few days, then drunk again, then sorry and sober for a little while longer.

It never changed.

But that is not the end of the story. I had been in the monastery almost seven years by the time I saw him again. Someone was in the guest parlor to see me, the sister who answered the door said. "He says he is your uncle," she added. But there had to be a mistake. I was on a small mission miles away from the monastery, and I certainly didn't have family in the area. I was slow going down the hall to the guest room. Whoever this was, I thought, had to be looking for someone else. I could see him standing there in the middle of the room, a little awkwardly, but strong and straight nevertheless.

It took a good long minute to figure out who he was, but suddenly I knew. And what was he doing here?

I don't remember a thing we said during that brief visit except for little snatches of conversation. I looked just like my father, he told me. He always admired my mother, he said. He was in Alcoholics Anonymous now and wanted to see all of us once more. He was trying to reconnect with everyone, trying to achieve some kind of rough relational parity for a lifetime's worth of lost personal ties. In fact, he had driven for hours that Sunday to see me. And then he said what I'll never forget: "I don't have much time to make up for everything I've done to my family," he said. "But I'm trying."

I never saw him again. He died less than a year later, dried up with cirrhosis of the liver. But the lesson he had come that day to teach me had come through loud and clear: life itself is the greatest spiritual discipline of them all.

Thanks to an exalted notion of human reason, we consider ourselves unassailable. Thanks to the linkage between natural disasters and the obsession with God's wrath, we look for reasons outside ourselves to explain our misfortunes. Thanks even to the scientific age, perhaps, and its insatiable thirst for technical advancement and its commitment to unstinting progress, we strive relentlessly for "progress" rather than personal fulfillment in the here and now. Thanks, indeed, to a peculiar brand of arrogance, humankind long ago fell victim to a most insidious form of spiritual heresy: the notion that there is such a thing as perfection and that humans are capable of achieving it.

The search for perfection, like a mite under the skin, goads us and drives us and makes us ill at heart when we fail to attain what we cannot possibly accomplish. But we raise the bar beyond the doable everywhere. We want "perfect 10s" in gymnastics, 300 hp engines in family cars, airplanes that fly faster than sound, multiple gigabyte processors in computers. We push every boundary to the breaking point — and in the case of cars and jet engines and desktop PCs sometimes we even get it. It's when we apply such standards to the human soul that things go miserably wrong.

Then we come face-to-face with the flat face of the soul, that part of us that grows only by increments and insights, never by trampolining from one self to another. This kind of change comes only slowly, only from one struggle to another, only barely.

The spiritual masters, given to whole lifetimes of confrontation with the self, knew it all too well. The monastics of the desert preserve for us the story of Abba Poemen and Abba John:

> Once upon a time, Abba Poemen said of Abba John that Abba John had prayed to God to take his passions away from him so that he might become free from care.
>
> "And, in fact," Abba John reported to him, "I now find myself in total peace, without an enemy."
>
> But Abba Poemen said to him, "Really? Well, in that case, go and beg God to stir up warfare within you again, for it is by warfare that the soul makes progress."
>
> And after that, when warfare came, Abba John no longer prayed that it might be taken away. Now he simply prayed: "Lord, give me the strength for the fight."

The story brings us up short. It is not perfect peace, Abba Poemen says, that is the acme of life. It is having the character, the commitment to muster up "strength for the fight."

Life confronts us always with our weakest selves. It is those parts we must come to understand, to own, to embrace. Some of us do it silently and secretly, if we do it at all. Others have no such luxury. They hang cruciform on their hungers, their emptiness, their compulsions, in the docks of the public square all their lives. And the rest of us, smug in our own perfection, judge them while they writhe.

But in their very embarrassment they hang there, public challenges to our private selves. They dare us to grapple, as they must do, with our own needs, our distorted desires all our lives. They beg us to find strength for the struggle, and finally, if we're lucky, to quietly, modestly, humbly admit to ourselves, at the very least, exactly who we are — and who we are not.

The real spiritual struggles of life are, more often than we care to know, the struggles of a lifetime. They are embedded in us like thorns in the flesh.

They are the recurring jealousies that curdle our souls with the acid of resentment.

They are the petty little angers that accumulate within us and then overflow into all the other areas of life, into our reactions to the demands of the children, to the insinuations of the in-laws, to the expectations of the workplace, even to the claims of those we love.

They are the lusts we damp down and struggle to smother — the cigarettes and alcohol, the food and the smut, the irrational wants and destructive desires that reemerge relentlessly — at the bar, at the computer, at the office, anywhere at all that we take our craving selves. And we always do.

The thing we fear to face, the thing we aren't told, is that the struggle with ourselves is the work of a lifetime. "What do you do in the monastery?" a disciple asked the monk. And the old monastic said, "Oh, we fall and we get up and we fall and we get up . . . and we fall. And we get up again."

It is not the time it takes us to come to grips with ourselves that is the measure of spiritual success. It is whether we ever really admit to ourselves who or what we are that counts. We may go on for years saying, "Well, that's the way I am." But it is only when we say to ourselves, "That is the way I am and for the sake of the rest of my world I must change" that we have really joined in the contest for our own souls. Sometimes it takes a lifetime before we even rally enough honesty to begin.

If the question is, What is wrong with me: why can't I change? the answer may be that I have to decide to begin. When the struggle will finally end, what the end will look like, we cannot know. We can only know that beginning to begin is the secret.

Chapter 20

What Is the Purpose of Life?

It was a cold day, one of those late fall days along the banks of Lake Erie when the rain is heavy, almost snow, cold to the bone. The Soup Kitchen is always over-full on those days. If the guests are not hungry they are chilled to the marrow. On those days, homeless people, jobless, some of them sick, all of them living out of shopping carts or garbage cans, come in off the streets and stay till it closes. It is, if nothing else, a place to warm up and talk a bit to the longtime staff, who call each of them by name before they leave the kitchen to face the long damp night alone.

The sister at the counter that day didn't really know the man in the long black overcoat all that well. He had come by a few times before with leftovers from an office party. A few times he simply walked up the steps, handed one of the sisters an envelope at the door, and left. Some days he dropped in and did some of the heavy work of filling the pantry shelves. This day he came in carrying hams to donate and, seeing the size of the crowd, stayed to fill plates in the serving line.

But it wasn't the sight of him serving salads that was so surprising that day. After all, some people make a regular ministry of it. Whole teams of them have come one day a week for years. Without them, the kitchen couldn't possibly survive. But this was different.

Just as he got ready to leave for the afternoon, coat on and scarf tight around his neck, he noticed that one of the guests sat at the end of the table, his legs pressed against the heating element, his summer sandals wet. Summer sandals. He was wearing summer sandals. He was wearing summer sandals with open toes and sling back heels over his bare feet. On the fringe of winter.

In a heartbeat, the man in the long black overcoat and silk scarf reached down, took off his shoes, handed them to the sister at the counter, and walked out. In bare feet. "Wait," she ran after him, "you can't go like that, without these. It's cold out there." The man kept moving down the street. "I know," he called back, "that's why I left them."

It's a story that has stayed with me for years. It is a true story. It really happened. A well-to-do man saw a homeless man in summer sandals on a cold day, bent over, took his own shoes off, and walked away barefoot.

Suddenly, all the words in the gospel, all the vocabulary I could muster about poverty and generosity, vacuity and purpose came together in one astounding, shocking act. And one even more difficult question: Was I prepared to do the same kind of thing? Was I prepared to give something away that would have more meaning, more import, to someone else than it did to me — especially when it did still have meaning to me?

The answer depends on whether we see ourselves as born for no reason at all, as kind of wastrel leeches on the globe who come, take what we can get, and, once surfeited on the goods of the earth, go. It has to do with whether we see ourselves as born with a mission in mind, unique to us, unfinished without us.

The way we are in the world depends on whether we know ourselves to be born to contribute to the dynamic spiral of life, born to augment its energy. What we do with our life depends on whether we see ourselves as essential to the network of existence, another hand-holder in the universe whose own life sustains the life of all the others just as they sustain mine. It depends on whether we see life, our life, ourselves, as beings with a function beyond breathing, not simply spun into being for the sake of the self alone.

The answer to why we're here, I suppose, lies in whether we see ourselves as the philanthropists or the venture capitalists of life, as meant to be moral agents in a dangerously immoral world or as speculators in a promising project called existence that has been designed purely for our exploitation. The choice we make between those two — between transforming life and exploiting the lives of others for our own benefit — makes all the difference to the kind of tomorrow we leave behind us when we go.

Venture capitalists give money away in order to make more money — and often do much good by their support of clearly questionable projects which, in the end, manage beyond all rational explanation to succeed. Philanthropists, on the other hand, simply give money away so that what must happen in the human condition can happen, whatever its improbability.

Philanthropists give the world art and music, hospitals and schools, libraries and research projects, youth centers and anti-poverty programs, with no hope whatsoever of recompense. They embody what it means to have purpose in life. They demonstrate what is implied in the Christian scriptures when the Book of Genesis says that the purpose of Adam and Eve is to "till the garden and keep it."

The purpose of life, the philanthropist knows, is to make the world better. The only question is, Why?

What the rest of us too often forget is that we are just as bound to give away our second set of shoes as the wealthy are. The data are clear: the garden we inherit, life as we receive it, like the garden in which Adam and Eve find themselves, is incomplete. Life is simply the responsibility of each of us to make our own contribution to the ongoing co-creation of the world.

The obligation of almsgiving is one of the oldest on the planet. Every major spiritual tradition has made almsgiving a cornerstone of spiritual existence. From the responsibility to "make merit" in the Hindu and Buddhist traditions to "Do unto others as you would have others do unto you" in the Abrahamic family, the spiritual demands of community support are a constant. Almsgiving is a plea to see ourselves as an essential element in the chain of life.

The monastics of the desert, known as hermits, who went to the desert to live as ascetics in isolation and abject poverty, nevertheless understood the social responsibility of the human enterprise quite clearly. The story they leave behind gives no room for any of us to excuse ourselves from the obligation to leave the world better when we go than it was when we found it.

Once upon a time, Abba Agathon was on his way to town to sell small baskets. On the way he saw a leper, crippled up and sitting on the roadside. "Where are you going?" the leper asked him.

"I'm going to town, to sell these things," Abba Agathon answered him, pointing at the baskets he had plaited to support himself.

Then the leper said, "Do me a favor and take me there." So Abba Agathon carried him to the town.

When they got there, the leper said, "Put me down wherever you sell your things."

So Abba Agathon put him down by the stall. And when he sold one item, the leper asked, "How much did you sell it for?"

When Abba Agathon told him the price that had been paid for the basket, the leper said, "Buy me something nice." So Abba Agathon bought something for him and sold another item.

Then, the leper asked again, "And how much was that one?" So Abba Agathon told him the price.

Then the leper said, "Buy me that thing over there now." So Abba Agathon bought the next thing for him.

After selling all his baskets, Agathon got ready to leave the market. Then, the leper asked, "Are you going back?"

"Indeed," said Abba Agathon. So the leper said, "Now do me a favor and take me back to the place where you found me."

So Abba Agathon put the leper on his back and carried him up the hill and back to the place where he found him.

Then the leper said to Abba Agathon, "You are blessed, Agathon, by the Lord — in heaven and on earth."

Then Abba Agathon raised his eyes, but there was no one there. Then he knew that it was an angel of the Lord who had come to test him.

The story challenges all the principles of modern society. What happens to independence here? What about rugged individualism? However can we justify the willingness of some to live off the labor of others?

But there are other principles of society that are just as strong, just as clear, that are being lost under the guise of self-sufficiency. What happens to community if we are not carrying those who cannot walk? What about our own hopes for interdependency when our houses are burning and our levees are breached and our crops have failed in the drought, if we have not mended the levees of all the others?

We are being sorely tested in a society where we call medical insurance for babies and daycare for working mothers and food stamps for underpaid families "welfare for the poor" but then fail to call agricultural subsidies and corporate bailouts and tax breaks for the wealthy "welfare for the rich."

We come into this world naked and alone. We grow on what others give us — the school system, the roads, the police protection, the garbage collection. None of us is totally self-sufficient. None of us really takes care of ourselves. None of us can lay our own roads, or provide our own security, or dispose of our own garbage, or supply all the computers and microscopes and teachers and books and basketball courts we need to compete on every level. We must all do together what none of us can do alone.

So, like Abba Agathon, we have a responsibility to do what we can for those who can do little or nothing for themselves.

The globe and all its people are in the hands of every succeeding generation. We are put here simply to provide another hand, another idea, another bit of support. We are here to take care of those who cannot take care of themselves while the rest of the world takes care of us, to do "for the least of these" so that the very life of a creating God can be honored in them.

If the question is, What is the purpose of life? the answer must be that the purpose of life for me is to be a life-giving part of it myself. Each of us has a crippled leper to carry whether we know them or not, whether we ever see them or not, whether we recognize them or not.

The world simply cannot do without us no matter what our level of society. We all have some kind of gift to give, some philanthropy to do. We have no right to default on the price of being human.

God did not finish creation. We are put here to do our part in completing the project. What else can possibly be worth a life?

Islamic Submission

CHAPTER 21

What Is There to Get Up for
in the Morning?

I first met Drew at an ecumenical gathering of rather erratic Christians who were neither regular churchgoers nor adamant non-believers. They functioned easily in mixed company, not because they didn't know anything about religion, but because they were neither convulsively skeptical nor rigidly neurotic about what they did know about it. They had no stomach for holy wars and, at the same time, no interest whatsoever in being proselytized. These were the kind of people who frowned on religious "fanatics" and took pride in their openness. These people were, if nothing else, a bridge between faiths.

These were not people who clung rigidly to past formulations of any faith. On the contrary, they walked easily at the edge of their traditions, their hearts willing, their souls full of spirit, their minds, on the other hand, full of perennial uncertainty, sometimes of downright doubt.

They had come to the point where they respected religion enough to know that they didn't know everything there was to know about anything. But they wanted to believe. And they did believe — in something. What was unclear to them, most of them, was precisely what that was.

Their problem, if it was a problem, was that they had long ago confused religion with faith. Faith, free-floating and tenuous, perhaps, but definitely real, they had. For them there was a God; God had created them; God wanted them to live good lives; God would hold them accountable for their actions, somehow, somewhere. Religion, meaning a particular or specific tradition that formed them, guided them, and rigidly defined the way they looked at life or lived in the world — this they lacked.

This kind of certain uncertainty or, better yet, uncertain certainty, would be seen by some, I'm sure, as both a blessing and a curse. Certainty is a blessing if it means that we know there is something beyond us, something worth seeking, something beyond either human arrogance or human desolation. On the other hand, certainty is a curse on the human race when it refuses to recognize, to respect, the equally sincere search of the world around it. One posture believes in a common mystery. The other insists on having all the answers to that mystery themselves.

I saw the faithful openness of this group simply as another kind of faith. These people were the searchers. They never totally believed everything they'd ever been taught, in the sense that they felt sure that a thing simply had to be true because they'd been taught it. But they never totally abandoned belief in the mystery of God's ways with us on earth either.

These people held God close to their hearts. They simply did not have the heart for defining one God over another. They doubted that any religion was the only religion that could guarantee their truisms.

Drew, however, was very different from the flock he pastored. He believed — and without a doubt. When I met him, he was a functioning Presbyterian minister, the deeply enculturated Scots kind. The real thing, in other words. Steeped in both his culture and his religion, it was sometimes difficult to know for sure whether he was more Scottish than Presbyterian or more Presbyterian than Scottish.

When I looked at Drew at the altar, I got the clear impression that I was looking at one of those rocks of the faith that every denomination writes hymns about. This was someone whom the rest of humankind sees and envies for their surety, someone not given to moments of total disbelief that sweep away years of Sunday school and a lifetime of faith, as are so many. On the contrary, in Drew they saw firmness of conviction. Drew's theological discussions fell on one end of the continuum or the other: an idea was either "true" or "false." There was no middle ground here. He was one of those believers who have absolute confidence that what they believe is right, is total, is complete, is ultimate. However much the difference and distance between those who believe without doubt and those who believe with hope alone, these are people to be esteemed when your own faith has more questions than answers.

But then it happened. The next time I saw Drew, a couple years later, he had left the Presbyterian ministry. Now he was an ordained Anglican clergyman. It was the liturgy he needed, he said. The sacramental system was just so much more revealing to him, he went on, than the more Puritan-inspired churches. Churches that set out to purify a person's relationship with God by stripping it of the pomp and circumstance, the mystery of the faith, the beauty and artistry of worship, he explained, were not enough to touch the soul at every level.

I thought about that for a while. It made me think about the different gifts of different religious streams even in the same tradition — Protestants, the Word; Catholics, the sacraments; the Orthodox, transcendence — and how they touch us differently. It was a sobering thought. How do we know where we belong, I thought? Why do we go on doing the same things all our lives, not only in religion but in everything else? And should we? What do we gain by such regularity? What do we lose?

Then I thought about Drew again. How is it that someone so seemingly intractable had become suddenly so fluid? What was faith anyway? And what was freedom?

They were interesting thoughts. Then I dismissed them for more important things, like how to get on with my own life.

It was at least another five years before I saw Drew again, this time at an interfaith conference of both Eastern and Western religions. I don't know how long we talked before I realized that there was some kind of gap in the conversation, some allusions I couldn't follow, some references that confused me. Drew was talking about patriarchs and icons. Finally, I put it together. Drew was now Greek Orthodox.

What do we do with something like that? Why does this man get up in the morning? Why do any of us get up in the morning? All these years I had thought it had something to do with finishing what we started in life, no matter how boring, no matter how difficult. What was Drew doing? Was this faithlessness at its most banal or faith at its most thoughtful?

For many, the whole scenario is simply unacceptable, if not incredible. How can one person embrace so many opposites in one lifetime? And yet, in a world of seeping borders and pluralistic states, of multiple options and shifting centers, of rapid change and unlimited social seductions, of new questions and new answers, the whole problem of unlimited possibility may be more common than we know.

Drew, after all, is not the only human being for whom the boundaries of life have been pushed to the breaking point. Other friends, in other arenas — professional, social, and geographical — have all done the same. Pat has three degrees — music, business, and theology — and can't seem to settle into the life of any one of them. Carol moves from place to place — Australia, Spain, Morocco, Japan — with all the aplomb of a global citizen to the point that nowhere now is really home.

Most important of all, perhaps, is the fact that for many who do not seem to move at all physically, there is within them the murmur of a restless soul. Nothing is quite right. Nothing fits completely. Nothing represents the wholeness of life.

The Sufis tell a story that may be a light to us all as we stumble along on our way, trying to find out, first of all, where we're going and second, how to really get there.

Once upon a time, there was a woman who had heard of the Fruit of Heaven. She coveted it.

So she asked a certain dervish, whom we shall call Sabar, "How can I find this fruit, so that I may attain to immediate knowledge?"

"You would be best advised to study with me," said the dervish. "But if you will not do so, you will have to travel resolutely and at times restlessly throughout the world."

She left him and sought another, Arif the Wise One, and then found Hakim the Sage, then Majzub the Mad, then Alim the Scientist. And many more. One after another after another.

Thirty years passed in her search. Finally she came to a garden.

There stood the Tree of Heaven, and from its branches hung the bright Fruit of Heaven.

Standing beside the tree was Sabar, the first dervish.

"Why did you not tell me when we first met that you were the custodian of the Fruit of Heaven?" she asked him.

"Because you would not then have believed me. Besides," the dervish went on, "the tree produces fruit only once in thirty years and thirty days."

And what can people like us, the staid and steady types, make of such a thing?

Life, the story tells us, is a mystery. But the mystery of it is inside of us at least as much as it is around us.

Like the woman in the story, we all want to know the secret of life. We want "immediate knowledge." Who am I? we want to know. What am I supposed to be doing? Where should I go? Who has the answers for me? What is it all about? What's really right? What's definitely wrong?

And like the woman in the story, we have two options.

The first option is an obvious one: we can wrestle with all those questions in whatever circumstances we find ourselves. We can study ourselves where we are, become alert to our feelings and our thoughts, our struggles and our irritations whatever we're doing, however things develop around us. We can become the students of our own reactions to the stagnant and the exciting. We can measure both the amount of balance and degree of excitement we show under stress. We can probe our motives and gauge our endurance against whatever standards we have.

Or there is a second option. We can try to answer the questions of life by pursuing every one of them. We can search the masters. We can seek out our gurus. We can refuse to take ourselves alone for a guide. We can move and run from one situation to another, dredge out of it all the truth we can, and when we have sucked it dry, go resolutely to the next, however incomplete the answers may be in us.

The fact is, the Sufi story implies, in the end it won't make much difference which option we choose. There is no quick fix, no "immediate knowledge" at all. Not in any arena, not even in religion.

Life is the mystery that takes a lifetime to solve.

The woman in the story does not want study. "You would be best advised," the dervish tells her, "to study with me." But introspection, reflection, contemplation, is not what the woman is interested in. What she wants is the fruit of the exercise, not the process. And so, she takes off in search of what her heart seeks and is restless to find.

She goes in circles for thirty years, the story tells us, and we smile at the thought of it. But don't many of us do the same, if not for everything, at least for one thing or another? We obsess with this and worry over that to the point of exhaustion. We become this or change that, but nothing really changes within us. The obsession continues. The worry never abates. The questions become perennial. We bring them up at every cocktail party. We ask them at every conference. We listen for the answers at every lecture. We buy one book after another, intent on finally finding the word, the phrase, the chapter that makes it all clear.

But running or staying in place, the calculus of living is the same: the essentials of life, the unchanging values of life, take time to find.

Reflection, the conscious commitment to exploring the caves of our own souls, patiently always, painfully if necessary, is one way to come to understand the essentials of life. Experience is the other. The very events of life can heighten our perception of them to the same degree as reflection. Kinneret Boosany, 23-year-old victim of a suicide bomber who spent four months in a coma and four years of surgery and rehabilitation, says of her life: "I can tell you I am more happy now with the person I am today than I was before the bombing. . . . There is more peace, more calm. There's less need to look around for stuff elsewhere. Now if I feel a lack of something I know I need to go into me — it's all inside. A lot of problems that I used to have then, I don't have them anymore. You know that you can get through anything."

But however long the reflection, whatever the experiences, the point of the story is not the search. The point of the story is that understanding, depth, awareness, and consciousness take time to develop in us as well as to find. "The tree produces fruit only once in thirty years and thirty days."

It is one thing to be told something. It is another thing entirely to come to know it, to own the truth of it ourselves.

If the question is, What is there to get up for in the morning? the answer is a simple one: we get up in the morning, go through one more boring or difficult, exciting or exhausting, restless or depressing day, in order to discover one more thing about life. Then, when we are ready — eventually, eventually — we will have learned what it is really all about.

CHAPTER 22

Where Is God?

Growing up in a Catholic school had a way of taking the grey out of life. Things verged on the absolute there. Starting as early as second grade, Sister made life pretty unequivocal.

Life, we came to understand, was divided into dos and don'ts, into non-negotiable rules and definite categories: forty days of Lent, seven capital sins, twelve gifts of the Holy Spirit, seven holy days of obligation, and three states of life. It was when we got to the three states of life that I really started to listen. This, after all, had to do with what you did when you got out of school. It marked the way you would spend the rest of your life on earth. You had to choose it yourself, but once you did, you were expected to do it forever.

It didn't take a lot of listening, however, to realize that the three "states of life" had a ranking to them.

The first state of life, "the highest vocation," was a commitment to the priesthood or to life in one of the religious orders. That, they told us, constituted a very special kind of life. That was life given totally to God, not to families or professions or personal pleasure. That was the real thing. That was a "vocation."

A vocation, they were careful to point out, was a call from God. We were all here on earth because God wanted us to do something. But some of us — the special ones — were wanted for something different. Anybody could be holy, of course, but total commitment to God, to the church, was something extraordinary, something unusually sanctifying.

The second state of life, the married state, was, well . . . normal. Most people, we all knew, would take this route. It was honorable, of course, but not quite, "quite." It was not, that is, quite as good or quite as holy as having a "vocation."

The third state of life — "the single life in the world" — got at best a sentence or two of consideration. And no wonder; almost no one ever heard of anyone doing it. In fact, I myself have met only two people in my life who did it consciously, who really believed that their call was to live alone all their lives, simply available to the world at large around them. Now, of course, U.S. census data tell us, more than nine million Americans live alone. How many of these do this for consciously chosen vocational reasons, and not because they are widowed, divorced, or still single but seeking marriage, is unknown. One thing is for sure: those for whom the single life is a vocation, a call to this particular state of life, is surely still small and definitely largely underdefined theologically and unencouraged vocationally. Little or nothing is said about "the single state of life" as something comparable to marriage or religious life on the scale of vocational choices, even yet — regardless of how many people are now living alone.

No one called it "the lowest vocation" in so many words, but everybody knew it was. No "vocation," no children, you didn't count for much.

So we all chose something. Or, even better, thought that it chose us.

These were the three "callings" from which a person could choose their destined place in life. If you really loved God, you could go to a religious order. If you weren't up to giving yourself to God, whole and entire, you could get married and have a family. If, for some unknown reason, you didn't want to do either, you could spend your life alone. But the third choice was risky. What kind of spiritual generosity was that? How close could you possibly get to God by living for yourself alone?

The theology of that kind of system shines because of its clarity. What's more, it's common to every tradition in some form or other. In every culture and spiritual value-system, those who devote themselves to the spiritual quest or direct others in such pursuits have a special place — and an important role — in the society. They keep the great spiritual questions of life uppermost before our eyes when we could easily sink into the easiness of the daily or get swamped by the immediate.

The problem with that kind of theology lies in the fact that it can lead to a class system based on a division of spiritual and ecclesiastical castes. In this case, vocations — single, married, and religious — came to be thought of as holy, holier, holiest. They were all acceptable, all of them sanctifying, of course, but some were more acceptable than others. They were all conducive to holiness, but some were innately holier than others, congenitally closer to God than others.

What's more, so exalted was the place of the religious vocation in the Catholic community that leaving it constituted a particular kind of faithlessness. People who left religious orders were branded for life. People whispered behind their backs, "He was a priest once, did you know?" Or, "Can you believe she was ever in a convent?" Ashamed of themselves for having left an order or a seminary, having "taken their hand from the plow," they were hesitant to tell anyone that they had ever been in a monastery at all. They lived embarrassed by their weakness, by their inability to live the special life and do the special work to which they had been "called." They had done the unthinkable: they had said no to God; they had given up "the sacred" for the secular; they had given up "holiness" for the mundane.

But the results of such thinking do not simply affect people who dedicate themselves to some kind of organized or institutionalized religious life. It can have an effect on those who do not take that path, too. It relieves them of the responsibility to aspire to great heights of holiness. Church and God become the purview of those who choose church vocations. Others simply go to church. Priests and nuns, sadhus and sadhi, ministers and rabbis, imams and Sufis in every tradition are the church, the mosque, the synagogue, the temple. They are the valiant ones. They are the ones to whom holiness naturally adheres like light to a candle, like perfume to incense. They are the "sacred" ones.

Such a theology colors the whole system. The notion that God is closer to some kinds of people than to others and that those other special kinds of people were, therefore, closer to God puts on some people an inhuman burden of perfection and on others the denigrating burden of spiritual limitations.

It's not surprising, then, to realize that most of the people canonized, by the Catholic Church, at least, have always been priests and nuns. We had all learned where to look for holiness, and it was not in the workaday world of mothers and fathers, sexual creatures all, mundane to the maximum.

Celibacy had become the defining characteristic of holiness, often to the diminishment of the sanctifying demands of sexuality for generosity, sacrifice, and the glory of co-creation. It blinded us, as well, to the valiant faith of single persons who gave themselves without restriction and without personal support to the needs of the world around them, regardless of relationship, regardless of personal risk.

The truth is that every major spiritual tradition, not Christianity alone, has singled out its spiritual seekers as models and guides, beacons and monitors of the essential questions of life. Swamis and gurus, monks and nuns, fakirs and priests all give themselves totally to the question of the sacred in the midst of the secular. And it is good for all of us that they do.

Like watchers in the crow's nest of the human night, they take the spiritual temperature of the world around them. They refuse to allow us to forget that there is more to being a human being than simply being human. They preserve for every age the spiritual questions that underlie life. Most of all, they become living flares of memory when the pressures of life crowd out the demands of the eternal.

But when life gets divided into two realms — into the sacred and the secular — and when being in one is more religious than being in the other, then religion itself has gone astray. The danger of religious professionals lies only in the temptation to make such people substitutes for our own striving.

When some make themselves the sole keepers of the spiritual life, they have failed — and so have we. When those people arrogate unto themselves the ultimate right to determine the character of holiness, become the overlords of the spiritual life, divide and define it for everyone else, then we stand to lose our own relationship with God. Then we lose our personal perspective on God, our own special sense of God in life. Then we risk surrendering the sanctity of the self by trading it for obeisance to the other. Then we hazard the possibility of forgetting where God really is. We begin to posit all grace and wisdom, goodness and holiness in someone else other than ourselves.

The Sufis deal with the problem with characteristic playfulness and profound disregard for anything that makes religious ritual more important than a personal relationship with God.

Once upon a time an old Sufi dervish set out to make the Great Pilgrimage to Mecca.

It was a difficult journey under any conditions. This particular year the trek was unusually demanding. The large crowds jostled one another and crowded him off the road. The path was rough and uneven. The sun beat down on the old man's head without mercy.

"I must stop for a while," the holy one decided.

So he lay down by the side of the road, just outside of Mecca.

He was hardly asleep before he felt himself being shaken roughly awake. "Sufi, get up," the imam said. The voice was not kind. The hand was not gentle.

"Some Sufi you are," the stranger went on. "You're a disgrace!"

The imam circled around the old man, flailing his hands and shaking his head.

"How dare you lie down at the time for prayer," he shouted, "with head turned to the West and your feet pointed toward God in the holy shrine."

The old Sufi stirred a bit, opened one eye, looked at the man, and smiled. "I thank you, sir, for your concern," the Sufi said. "So before I go back to sleep," he went on, a grin playing at the corner of his mouth, "would you be so kind as to turn my feet in some direction where they are not pointing at God?"

The story ends, leaving us with a new awareness of the old Sunday school dictum: Where is God? God is everywhere.

Everywhere. Not simply in those things designated by humans as sacred but most of all in those things designated by God as human — in one another, yes, but in the self as well. If we live consciously in touch with the God within, there is simply no without. If we insist on touching the God-life we feel in the depths of the self, every day we grow more godly. If we search inside ourselves as well as outside ourselves — and outside ourselves as well as inside ourselves — to find God, we come to recognize that God is everywhere.

The story has a great deal to say about holiness. Holiness, we learn, is the byproduct of immersion in the God who is everywhere.

First, it is obvious that simply going through the rituals of religion does not make anybody holy. On the contrary. That may be exactly what fuels the pride that betrays the superficiality of our spirituality. The Sufi's fellow pilgrim knew everything about the protocol of the pilgrimage but little about the compassion of God or the Muslim's obligation to care for the other.

Second, it is equally clear that the Sufi knew himself to be human and embraced his humanity with all its limitations. There were no airs put on here, no affectation, no posturing. The Sufi had walked the rough road with all the other pilgrims to the Haj, expecting no special attention, asking for no privileges, seeking no dispensation from the journey. He did not separate himself from the rest of humankind. He did not put himself on a higher level than those around him. He did not pretend to be what he was not.

He was a person who had spent his life looking for God the best way he knew how. He was not special; the way was not special. He simply carried within himself a living magnet that directed his life and calmed his heart. The God who made us, he knew, expects no more of us than what we are. But he does expect that we are striving.

Finally, the Sufi teaches, with all the saints and mystics of the world — in the boldest way possible — that God is not a thing to be made captive to our pious coaxings. God, "the merciful, the compassionate," however good and beneficent, is not a puppet on a prayer string. If God is the very origin of our lives and the support of our existence, then God is our companion on the way, the air we breathe, the thoughts we think, the ocean of the Spirit in which we move.

The presence of God is not dependent on ecclesiastical rank of any kind or ilk. The presence of God does not reside in who or what we think we are. Instead, it lodges in what we carry within us.

Only the aggrandizement of the self can block the presence of God within us. Only the consciousness of the omnipresence of God can enable it. If God is everywhere, then the locus of God is both within us and around us at the same time. And if God is not everywhere, how can God possibly be God?

It is only when we make God a thing, when we put God somewhere and call the mundane sacred, that we make God inaccessible. When God is confined to only some parts of society, the presence of God is made a laughingstock. When God-talk is made the special information of only some few of the faithful, God is stolen from the people. When holiness is compartmentalized or made subject to hierarchies of piety, then the rest of creation becomes foreign land to God.

Marks of the sacred in place and people are, at best, only reminders that God is in front of our blind eyes while we try to make God visible.

There are those, of course, who need to believe that God is beyond their reach, outside their grasp. Otherwise, they themselves are accountable to make that God present wherever they are. There is nothing more stunning than to realize that the quality of the God-space around us depends on what we ourselves bring to it. It takes the joy out of complaining about the quality of the society in which we live. It shocks us into understanding, as Gandhi said, "Be the change you want to see in the world"; as we are so shall the world be.

If the question is, Where is God? the answer is distressingly uncomplicated: God is wherever we know God to be, wherever we bring God to be, no more and no less at any time, anywhere, or in anyone.

Chapter 23

What Is Happiness?

For the first time in history, happiness has become a commodity. Western advertising sells it, clinicians promise it, mental health personnel test for it, drug companies bottle it, researchers study it. Shangri-La, that place of absolute satisfaction and perfect serenity, remains the holy grail of an affluent world.

But all that has really been learned in the process is that the one thing money can't buy is happiness.

Most confusing of all, perhaps, is that comparative studies of multiple happiness surveys taken in the last decade indicate that more people have actually described themselves as less happy in recent years than before. We have reached, apparently, what researchers have called "the stagnation of happiness." According to researchers for the World Values Survey reported in the UK's *New Scientist* magazine, happiness levels have changed little since the end of World War II despite the fact that incomes have continued to rise in startling proportions.

What is even more interesting is the fact that people are now reporting that it is not the absolute level of their salaries that determines their degree of happiness but the value of their income relative to the income of others — which means that it really isn't income that makes people happy at all. It's success. It's not just keeping up; it's having a little more than the Joneses. It doesn't mean much, it seems, to own a Jaguar if nobody thinks it's important. It means even less if everybody else has one, too.

It's winning the achievement game that's played secretly, within the heart of the player, that's important. It's winning the competition that no one knows about that seems to determine how people feel about themselves and the quality of their lives.

It is, in other words, the fear of losing the game of life, of being left behind, of being embarrassed, humiliated, labeled a "failure," that people use to determine the happiness quotient of their lives.

But it may also be the problem of inflated expectations that makes economic well-being relative and happiness illusory. People may be reporting less happiness because they are not winning as much as they expect. It may simply mean that economic conditions can continue to improve for some and at the same time cease to make people happier. If they get more — but get less than they expected to get or wanted to get or needed to get in order to surpass the people around them — they are not yet happy with what they have, no matter what they have. Tragic.

The drug "happiness" may, apparently, be addictive. The more we have, if having things is the way we compare ourselves to the rest of our world, the more things we will need to sustain it. Things and happiness become synonyms. Except that, obviously, they aren't. But there are no warning labels in a consumerist, capitalist world, telling the user to beware confusing the two. On the contrary. We actually work at connecting them, however incorrect and illusory that may be. The link is everywhere. Advertisers create false needs to spin the consumer wheel that makes capitalism work. And yet, it seems, it does not work, at least not where happiness is concerned.

It is a hapless, hopeless circle. What's more, it is apparently a useless one.

What happens if and when the salary level has been reached, or salaries, in a time or place of price and wage caps, cease to go up? What happens to the soul of a person when the economic gods of our generation fail to function? Like Baal on the plain with the prophet Elijah, who appealed to false gods to turn wet wood into fire, the god money seduces us into thinking that "having it all" is really having it. But the real question is, What is it that we really have when all we have is money?

If there was ever a measure of the difference between the United States and most of the rest of the world, it is in the magnitude of difference between the happiness scores of one country and another. In a world where comparing ourselves to others is the quicksand on which we base our sense of well-being, the comparison between national happiness indices demands a very different approach to happiness than twenty-first-century economics are apparently able to provide.

The happiest country in the world, the World Values Survey, conducted approximately every four years, tells us at the beginning of a whole new century of grasp and grabbing, is Nigeria, followed by Mexico, Venezuela, El Salvador, and Puerto Rico. Obviously, the things we buy and own and accumulate and hoard and display to the world as signs of our success cannot possibly be what happiness is about in places like this. Obviously, it is possible to be happy without them.

But if that is the case, then what is happiness really about?

Respondents to the World Values Survey from around the world, when asked what they thought were the paths to happiness, ranked money eighth out of the top ten factors in the list of necessary elements of happiness. Eighth.

It's easy to assume that people who do not have money might discount money as a happiness factor simply because they do not have it. But if the people who do — the United States, Britain, Australia, the Netherlands, Switzerland, Canada, and Japan — rank behind poor countries, the conundrum is even clearer: even the rich don't see their riches as a bulwark against unhappiness.

The United States ranked sixteenth out of sixty-five countries of the world in happiness. India, one of the poorest countries of the world, ranked sixth. Ghana and Latvia, Croatia and Estonia all ranked above the U.S., too.

So what is happiness? Even knowing that money is not it, it's still not possible to know what it is. Happiness surveys, after all, can be very skewed by the lack of a common definition. Or they can be affected by the mood of the moment, or by the state of the nation at any given time, or even by expectations that loom at the time of the survey but in the end never come to pass.

So, in effect, even answers from people who call themselves happy are anything but foolproof, anything but certain. But, in general, when asked what makes for happiness, respondents say things that would surprise some, annoy others.

The response that ranked first in the survey was a simple one: some personality types are simply genetically predisposed to be happy, many said. Happiness they saw as a function of our genes. You either have it or you don't. You're a happy personality or you're not.

Marriage claimed second place as a happiness factor. Being loved, knowing ourselves to be cared for, and having some kind of emotional security ranked high among the poorest of peoples.

Making and valuing friends — marriage or no marriage — ranked third. The notion of a wider circle of support than simply family ties in a world where families are more likely than ever to be far-flung loomed large. Other people, it seems, have a lot to do with our happiness.

Desiring less to begin with ran a strong fourth. "What the eye cannot see, the heart cannot grieve," the saying goes, and such a philosophy seems to be deeply embedded in people around the world. What we don't allow ourselves to want, we can't be unhappy about not having. The kind of heartache that implies for a consumer economy built on false needs and fabricated desire can hardly be ignored.

Doing someone else a good turn and having religious faith took fifth and sixth positions in the happiness marathon. Believing that in caring for others we ourselves are cared for, believing that there is some good, some benevolent God, in all the bad in our lives, becomes a lifeline when life is tenuous at best. When there is nothing we can do for ourselves, the only thing to do is to hope that help will come from somewhere else.

And finally, the strength even to stop comparing our looks with the looks of others, to stop living on the public dock of social standards, to stop being eaten away inside by what we want to look like but do not, exceeded the place of money in the happiness index of the modern world. Not to want to be brown if you're white, or white if you're black, perhaps, or tall if you're short, all counted more than money in the bank to people.

And yet, in the end, are any of those things, let alone money, enough? And if not, what is happiness all about? It is the eternal question, the universal issue. And if spirituality has ever dealt with it, what does it have to say to a world that has tried wealth and found it lacking?

The Sufis tell a story that rings in every spiritual tradition around the world:

Once upon a time, a powerful king, ruler of many domains, was in a position of such magnificence that wise men were his mere employees. And yet one day he felt himself confused and called the sages for a consultation.

He said to them: "I do not know the cause, but something impels me to seek a certain ring, one that will enable me to stabilize my state.

"I must have such a ring. And this ring must be one which, when I am unhappy, will make me joyful. At the same time, if I am happy and look upon it, I must be made sad."

The wise men consulted one another. They threw themselves into deep contemplation. Finally they came to a decision as to the character of the ring that would suit their king.

The ring that they devised was one upon which was inscribed the words: THIS, TOO, WILL PASS.

It is enough to make anyone pause. What I have now, I will someday not have. What is bothering me now will end, and I will not be bothered by it in the future. So, if I can hold my world, all of it — good and bad, exciting and terrifying, exhilarating and tragic — with open hands, nothing will ever be able to destroy me. Neither having too much and so wasting it, nor having too little and grasping for more, can possibly be the albatross that shadows me to the end.

Happiness comes when clinging goes. We are all misers. What we have, we try to keep. What we do not have, we die to get.

When we are doing what we like, we try to freeze in time our right to do it. Like hamsters on a wheel, we insist on running in place however much the world around us goes on changing.

We try to commandeer friends, buy them with gifts or favors, privileges or power. But whatever the garnish, they move naturally away — either to be themselves or to get more from someone else some other place. And we lie crushed in the dust of rejection while they pursue their own goals and other stars, not us.

We make every attempt to hold on to power that is for its own time only. We fail to understand that power is ultimately what we have within us, not the positions we get. Some people in power have no internal power at all. No position makes them powerful; it simply puts them in power. Eventually, ironically, either the position ends or they live powerless in the position.

We try to hold on to past gains and so lose the opportunities of the present moment. We refuse to move on and so cement ourselves in the past. We get out of touch. We become a remnant of times long gone.

Then, the Sufis tell us in the story of the king who had no need of anything, the only way to be happy is to understand that whatever is our state at the present moment, this moment is already over. There is no amount of pain, no depth of pain, no disturbance or joy or irritant or exhilaration or suffering, that can possibly last forever. To be happy we must come to understand that. "This, too, will pass."

Tomorrow is another day made for me to shape and enjoy, bear and endure, let go of and move on. What we do not seek to control or to avoid cannot possibly make us unhappy.

If the question is, What is happiness? the answer must be that happiness is the ability to live every day, every phase, every stage of life in the awareness that it will not be ours forever — and that is just as it should be if we are to grow and live, live and grow.

CHAPTER 24

What's Important in Life?

A number of things that morning made me uncomfortable — first, the newspaper headlines, then the CNN radio news.

In the first place, the headlines told me four things: (1) 1,500 people had just been buried in a mudslide caused by logging activities on the mountain above their village; (2) we were back to the point where the United States was arming one puppet-state and the Soviet Union was arming another one against them; (3) a cleric somewhere offered a $1 million bounty for the assassination of a cartoonist; and (4) the Powerball Lottery had reached a record high of $365 million.

In the second place, CNN business news reported that college graduates with degrees in computer engineering can plan to get a starting salary that is anywhere from $25,000 to $30,000 more than liberal arts majors or psychologists can hope to earn.

Something about all of that jars the soul. Are these the things life must really be all about? And if they are, what about the people to whom these tragedies are happening or the people who will not be making the salaries at the upper end of the scale, let alone winning the lottery?

What will their lives be like? Or to put it another way, what, if anything, can take the edge off the brutal parts of life so that no matter how brutal life is, we can live through it without bitterness, beyond despair, with a relaxed grasp? Is there a way to make the journey through life more livable, more humane, more meaningful?

It is surely no accident that religious literature from every tradition uses "journey" as a universal spiritual metaphor for human life. The truth is, they're right. None of us is born finished. No life is completely static, even if it is lived in the same place doing the same things for an entire lifetime. No life escapes the gains and losses that come with being human.

Life has multiple phases, each deeper, more mysterious than the one before. Just when we think we're finally "on our way" — whatever that means — the road pitches and changes, takes a sudden turn, or simply meanders to a place we never wanted to go to or expected to be.

We struggle from one period to the next, or we float for so long in some kind of directionless orbit that life seems to stall or quit along the way.

But there is no such thing as stalling or quitting. In every state and stage of life, there is something going on underneath, a kind of universal restlessness or query: What's it all about? What do I really want? What should I be concentrating on — money, fame, power, position, security, order, what? Do I want to be a clever businessman, a good father, a faithful wife, an influential citizen, a beach bum, a career woman, a scholar? And if I manage any of them, what's left over when those things end? In fact, is there anything left over at all, from one stage to the next?

What will really be important when all the important things fade?

Youth is important. It's the period of life when everything is possible. Young energy never fades, never ends. We party till 4:00 a.m., sleep till midday, and then get up and start over again. And there's time in which to do it. There's always a sense of unlimited time for us when we're young. We have nothing but time, we think, in which to shop around through life till we can find what we like and pluck it.

The problem with youth is that it has no grasp of the wholeness of life and must therefore stumble from pit to pit, from grace to grace.

Beauty is important. The flush of *savoir faire* that comes with the right piece of jewelry, the excellent cut of the coat, gives an unfathomable feeling of security. People stop and look, admire and are attracted. We spend a lot of time, a lot of money being beautiful. It must be important.

The problem is that beauty shifts as life goes by from the outside of us to the inside of us. Real beauty is not what we're born with; it's what we become. Otherwise, when cosmetics and haircuts can no longer camouflage either the wrinkles or the grey, there's nothing left to attract, to amaze, to overawe the other.

Money is important. It gives us the right to move on in life. It reeks of the competence it took to get it, to keep it. It signals and makes life sweet. It buys travel and experience, friends and distance, comfort and self-sufficiency.

The problem is that money can only give us things. The friends we buy with it disappear as it disappears. When the money goes, they go. Or if not that, they change with the house, the job, the circles we join, the vagaries of life.

Relationships are important. A woman on the arm, a man to depend on, a friend for fun, and a set of connections that oil our path through life can be the ultimate status symbol. And if not a status symbol, at least the ultimate confidence-builder in strange situations.

But relationships built on social affectation and public networks seldom last through the hidden parts of life. When the pain and dust of maintaining the relationship come, these friends find themselves another connection, a more stunning exhibition of the self. They surface for the show of it and vanish when the show ends.

Security is important. Anything can happen to anyone at any time: sickness, unemployment, even an attack of whimsy that sets us off in a bad direction, interesting as it may be at the beginning, can skew the best-laid plans for life.

But security is a dull companion. It speaks of the staid and the safe. It augurs against risk and exploration. It cautions us at all times. It warns us not to go too, too far in life lest we find ourselves living on sand and water. It admonishes us not to be seduced by life.

Power and influence are certainly important. They are the elixir of life. They make things happen, yes, but more important than that, at least in some situations, they make me feel significant. They are the taste of success that comes with a life lived out of a surfeit of ambition.

But power is something people live through; it is seldom something that can be banked. Presidents live to be ex-presidents; governments come and go. Today's headline is tomorrow's memory.

Clearly, life is fugitive, fleeting. Like mercury, it slips through our fingers before we even think to bottle it. So, on what shall we spend our life? What can sustain us in the course of life and comfort us at life's end?

And how can we be sure?

Every major religious tradition deals with the nature and purpose of life. For all of them, it has something to do with liberation or release from the bondage of the body and all its pains and strife.

At the same time, there is the question of how to make good life decisions, or how to compensate for bad ones while we're here.

There is a need to define the priorities of life no matter how much of the other dimensions of living — beauty, relationships, security, influence, and money-making — must be, should be, organized around them. In fact, setting life priorities for ourselves is often the most difficult thing to do. Making decisions about all the little things we will do with our lives out of all the possible things that life has to offer is one thing. Deciding what we want to become as a person as we do them is entirely another. What we will spend our lives doing is often a far less important question than what we want to end up being while we do whatever it is we do with however much time we have.

Great spiritual traditions all warn us to make a distinction between the two. The Sufis, for instance, tell us this story:

> Once upon a time, there was an elder who was respected for his piety and virtue. Whenever anyone asked him how he had become so holy, he always answered, "I know what is in the Qur'an."
>
> Once he was discovered sick unto death but completely without complaint. "How did you manage to stay so calm in such a situation?" his disciples asked him.
>
> "I know what is in the Qur'an," the old Sufi said.
>
> Later, the old man was robbed of everything in his cell, even his bed roll and candles. "How did you keep your temper?" they asked him.
>
> "I know what is in the Qur'an," the old man answered them.
>
> One season no figs grew, and the old man almost starved to death.

"How could you possibly have managed to survive?" the disciples asked in awe.

"Because I know what is in the Qur'an," the old man said.

So when the old man died, they raced one another to his hut to find out for themselves what was in his Qur'an. "Well, what is it?" they shouted.

The disciple holding the book looked up from it amazed and said with wonder in his voice, "What is in this Qur'an are notes on every page, two pressed flowers and a letter from a friend."

There are some things in life, whatever its burdens, however it is spent, which if we cultivate them will never die, will be the source of our joy forever, will sustain us through everything.

"Two pressed flowers," beauty off the bloom, memories of past good days, remain in memory and heart long after the event has ended. Beauty scatters seeds of hope in us. It reminds us of time that was good for its innocence. It brings us face-to-face with the natural. It reminds us that, like the seasons, whether we want this present moment or not, it has a place in our growth that in the end will flower forth in ways we cannot now see.

This is the kind of beauty that is not bought and not cultivated, not clung to and not hoarded. It refuses to call the pornographic in life "beautiful." It reminds us that we live in the Garden we are meant to tend, not destroy. It raises us to see in ourselves the ability to create beauty as we go and to expect beauty from the Creator whether we can always see it at first glance or not.

"Two pressed flowers" become the treasury of those moments in time when spontaneous laughter made a moment rich and unforgettable. They echo on in life long after the moment ends and ring a reminder to us of the incessant, bedrock beauty of life, however long or many its sad days. They remind us that there is in life, down deep, and unexpectedly, an essential basic and beautiful goodness that redeems all the moments we ourselves overlay with greed or hatred or anger or self-centeredness.

The holy life cultivates those moments. They are the heartbeat of the universe. They make us glad to be alive. They hold us up in hope when everything around us seeks to drown us in despair.

They remind us, whatever the tenor of today, that we have known beauty once and can find it again.

"Notes in the margins of our scriptures" lift us above the mundane and make us look again at what we are, at what we are called to be. They require us to be reflective about what we do and why we do it. They remind us that there is a greater purpose to life than simply making a living. Reflection — this conscious comparison of the goals and hope of my life with all the possible purposes of life — gives us a new sense of the nobility of life. It stretches us to be everything we can be, in even the worst of circumstances. It refuses to remain mired in the search for power and security that isolate us from the rest of humankind.

Reflection on the great questions of life puts everything else into perspective. We are meant to be about more than money and social craftiness. We are called to be more than simply passers-by in life. We are here to strive for the best in us, to reach into the center of us, to remember that we are decidedly human and decidedly more than that at the same time. We have within us the stardust of the universe, and we are on our way home.

Nothing smaller than the cosmos is meant to distract us from a God's-eye view of life.

Finally, friendship — love — "letters from our friends," touch us so that we might eventually learn to touch others. We come to this world from the moment of birth unable to function without the help of others. We grow, then, into that purpose ourselves: to care for those around us so that, caring for one another, we may all live secure in the knowledge that we are safe and wanted, necessary and loved.

Our letters remind us that it is what and whom we have loved which, in the end, shapes the quality of our lives.

When all the stages of life have passed us by, these things alone remain: the spiritual treasure that stretches our souls to see what our eyes cannot, the remembrance of how beautiful life really is under all its ugliness, and the love of those around us who make the journey gentle as we go.

If the question is, What things are really important in life? the answer depends on what is in the Qur'an that is your heart.

To make the journey of life and cultivate none of those things is to squander our years. Anything less is pure chimera. We grasp for mercury and morass when we concentrate only on cosmetic beauty and transient power, for social connections and uncertain security. Those things are all real, of course, even necessary. They are part of all our lives at one time or another. But they deceive. They only come and go. They are running through our fingers like water through a strainer, even as we speak.

If the question is, What is really important in life? the answer is only life itself, living it well, immersing it in beauty, love, and reflection.

CHAPTER 25

Why Do I Feel That Something Is Missing in My Life?

She was a middle-aged woman, a grandmother, in fact. She had raised seven children alone after her husband left her. They were grown now, all of them on their own. "I've done everything I can for them," she said. "Now it's my turn." I looked at her closely. This was a woman who should be going into retirement, I thought to myself. She should be settling down to wait for the visits, the grandchildren, the invitations to a Thanksgiving dinner which, for the first time in forty years, she did not have to cook. "And what are you going to do for yourself?" I asked. "I'm going back to school," she said. "I want to know something."

HE WAS A successful businessman from a family with an even more successful farm. The land alone was worth thousands of dollars per acre, and they owned miles of it. He was in his 40s. He lived alone in the great large house on the top of the hill that he and his wife had built together before she died. "Something's missing in my life," he said. "Time will dull the edge of the pain," friends promised him. "Then someone will come along. Don't worry. You're young yet."

But it never worked for him. No other marriage could replace the first one, he told them. It wasn't marriage he was looking for now. "But what else is there?" the family said. "Everybody else," he said and applied to a monastery in the South somewhere.

"I DON'T KNOW what to do with my life," the young woman said. "I'm just not sure yet." She had graduated in art and then gone on to be a nurse. It all worked and nothing worked. No place seemed to make the perfect fit between what she could do and what she wanted to do, between what she was and what was missing in her life.

It took years of trying. Her art succeeded as far as art can for a young person, but she couldn't make a living that way. So she tried nursing and did very well. But it wasn't enough. For a while she taught, but that didn't really satisfy her either. Eventually she went back to school for a degree in theology and began to work with college students on a nearby campus. Finally, she went to a convent for several years, but when that training period ended, she decided to leave. There was simply something missing in her life, she said. But who knew what?

They called her a rolling stone.

But I began to wonder whether we aren't all the same.

SOMETHING IN all of us strains for fulfillment. Some people spend their lives attempting to find it. They move eagerly from experience to experience. Nothing ever really seems to do it. But they keep looking anyway.

Others, though, roll like glaciers, slowly and ponderously, deeper and deeper into themselves as the years go by, becoming more and more taut, more and more quiet about life. They live it. They go on. But, far too often, they simply fail to thrive. They get to the point where they are simply living it out. Then, however much they go on breathing, they have stopped living. And they know it.

The missing element in life echoes like a chorus across the land. "If only we had a car, I could. . . ." Or, "If only I had gone to school. . . ." Or, "If only I had not gotten married. . . ." "If only . . . if only . . . if only."

There comes a point in life when, having stopped living, we decide that life is simply a sour kind of trap and we are in it. We look out from where we are like butterflies behind a plexiglass screen. We cling to life, but we never explore beyond it. As a result, we can see what we're missing and we resent it, but we do nothing about it.

The *London Daily Mail* carried an article years ago that ought to be a warning to us all. It went like this:

Once upon a time, not so very long ago, a certain building became infested by mice. The people in charge decided to exterminate them.

One night they put down mouse-killing poison, and the next morning the poison had been eaten, but there were no dead mice in sight.

The people changed the poison and made a second attempt. But this second dose the mice also ate and left signs that they were thriving on their new diet.

This time, the people decided to use old-fashioned, spring-operated mousetraps. They baited them with thick pieces of succulent cheese.

But the mice refused to touch the cheese.

One of the mouse-catchers suddenly had an idea: he coated the cheese in the traps with poison. "Perhaps the mice have developed a liking for poison," he said. "It may even be doing them good," he reasoned.

The following morning the spring-traps were full of what once had been strong and healthy mice.

This story, the article ended, is absolutely true.

The fear is, of course, that we can all learn to live on what is poisoning us. We might, conceivably, even appear to thrive on it. "It's good for us," we tell ourselves and engorge ourselves on it. Eventually, totally unaware that what we are cemented in is killing us slowly or saturating us to the point that whole other parts of ourselves are silently dying instead, we simply get up every day and keep on going to nowhere that's really good for us.

Too much of a bad thing may be just as addictive as too much of a good thing. Too much of anything stifles our taste for the rest of life or exhausts our capacity to pursue it. What's more, it is almost impossible to tell one from the other. Each of them deceives us. Each of them intoxicates us to the point that we can no longer save ourselves from either of them. But somewhere in the dark center of ourselves we always know that "something is missing from our lives."

It's the missing part that must be attended to while we still have enough life left in us to respond.

When life is lived on the physical level alone, when we bound through life like children at a candy counter, grabbing up sensations, living for the sensual, and at the same time having gone dead to stimulation of any kind

— when it always takes another drink, another laugh, another injection of bloodshed or action or sex to keep us high — we live wrung-out lives. There is nothing left to assure us that we are, indeed, alive. Then we know that something is missing.

When we live life solely in our heads, in some stratosphere of thought without a body, without ever coming down out of the desiccated air of old ideas, we make a travesty of thought. Thought, the ancients knew, was intended to make the world better. The function of thought was not simply to preserve the past. It was not meant to mummify the human heart in bloodless ideas of ethereal nothing. Thoughts were not meant to be mounted like specimens on a wall. When the thoughts we think are nothing but a museum of old ideas and attitudes — long dead but not gone — then the human side of life is missing.

When we fail to nourish the soul, to challenge it to its heights, we deny it the right to be. We neglect to let it breathe in the spirit of the rest of the world. We make of the rest of humanity a vessel empty of meaning, hollow of heart. Then we overlook the wisdom of the ages, the pulse of life that beats in the universe and waits still for our finding. Most of all, we condemn ourselves to a life lived below its inherent potential. We become sentient creatures rather than spiritual beings, thinking puppets rather than reflective individuals.

The missing part of us is what the spiritual life is all about. And every great spiritual tradition has always known that. "I fear that you will not reach Mecca, O Nomad," Saadi of Shiraz once wrote, "for the road that you are following leads to Turkestan!" We can't get what we don't aim for in the right places, by the right means. We cannot fill ourselves up with worthlessness and expect to find what is missing in us, or, even worse, to know in time how much we are really missing. We are restless for a reason.

So what is the use of restlessness?

The Sufi tell a teaching story that may explain to all of us how it is that we find our way by losing it.

Once upon a time, a man came to the great teacher Bahaudin.

He asked for help in his problems and guidance on the path of the Teaching.

To everyone's surprise, Bahaudin, one of the most respected spiritual teachers of the time, simply told the man to abandon spiritual studies and to leave his court at once.

A kind-hearted visitor who saw the encounter began to remonstrate with Bahaudin. "Why would you do such a thing, Master?" he asked. "The man was seeking help and you denied him. He wanted to know what to do and you refused to help him. He is unsure of his future and you did not listen to his concerns."

But Bahaudin only smiled. "You shall have a demonstration of the Teaching," said the sage.

Just at that moment a bird flew into the room, darting hither and thither, not knowing where to go in order to escape.

The Sufi waited until the bird settled near the only open window of the chamber and then suddenly clapped his hands.

Alarmed, the bird flew straight through the opening of the window — to freedom.

Bahaudin looked at the well-meaning visitor. "To the suppliant the sound of that answer must also have been something of a shock, even an affront, do you not agree?" asked Bahaudin and bowed.

It was, the Sufi teaches us, the shock of the clap that drove the bird out of Bahaudin's window. And, in like manner, the spiritual teacher Bahaudin explains, it is the shock of finding ourselves alone and in confusion that can drive a seeker into that reservoir of self where the answers to the future have been long germinating. To put the seeker through years of useless discussion in an attempt to discover what he already knew, Bahaudin implies, would be, at best, a waste of time. To allow the seeker to make life nothing but an academic question — however holy it might seem — rather than a real quest for real fullness would not be spiritual guidance. It would be, at most, a spiritual play school. Only the conscious awareness that something was missing in his life that some change in him and him alone could supply would eventually drive him to find it.

It is so easy for us to do the same. We go from one teacher to another, one spiritual exercise to another, one spiritual experience to another, one spiritual fix to another, looking for someone to tell us an easy way, a painless way, to do what we know can only be done with effort.

All of us deal with the temptation in life to settle down where we are, doing what we're doing, no matter how dry the nest, how wrong the tree. We are too often inclined to stay on the same shrub long after the berries that brought us there are gone for us. We assume that one part of life can nourish us forever, and we let the rest of ourselves remain unnurtured for years.

Then we wonder why it is that the things that once upon a time gave us great delight now stir nothing in us at all. We are at a loss to know how it can be that life has gone grey for us. We want others to tell us what to do and where to go rather than striking out on our own, aware that we are looking for the piece of us that has been yet unattended to.

If the question is, Why does it feel like something is missing in my life? the answer is because the feeling of emptiness is meant to move us on beyond where we are now to the fullness of life we are only here to discover.

EPILOGUE:

THE ROOTS OF TRADITION

Each of the great spiritual traditions — Hinduism, Buddhism, Judaism, Christianity, and Islam — has multiple variants of one basic message. They spring from the same kind of spiritual impulse and seek the same kinds of spiritual things — peace, transcendence, freedom of soul. But they often do it with subtle variations in custom or practice.

Those historical mutations are not the subject matter of this book, interesting and important as they are.

This book is about the kind of wisdom that has emerged out of the well of the ages of each tradition that has something yet to say to our own age.

In the pages that follow, I have attempted to define one or more of the major facets or defining charisms of each tradition. My hope is simply to provide some kind of context for the stories themselves for those who have little or no contact with the broader tradition.

For more serious, in-depth study, I would suggest that the reader pursue one of the many comparative religion texts now being used in schools and study groups everywhere or, even more important, perhaps, one of the major interpretive texts that not only describe the practices of a particular faith but set out to interpret the meaning of each faith for its devotees.

World religion is one of the keys to universal community in our time. It has a great deal to teach us all. More than that, it has a great deal to tell us about how the other parts of humanity think and why.

Religion, often the cause of worldwide division and danger, ironically is meant to be the glue that binds us together as a human race. But for that to happen, we must all come to know, understand, and respect the other as well to take from all the very best answers they have to offer to the questions in our own lives.

CHAPTER 26

Hindu Wisdom and Eternal Meaning

Once upon a time, in India, thousands of years ago, hard as it may be to believe, life — real life, the kind of life that takes place in the very center of a person — was actually not very different from our own, not spiritually or interiorly or philosophically.

Certainly everything looked different on the outside, of course. Life was raw and rough and rugged then, not technological or wired or comfortably institutionalized. But on the inside, at the heart of people, ironically enough, things were very much the same, emotions were very much the same. The social situation was very much the same. People were confused and wary. What had forever, it seemed, been unquestionable had suddenly been cast into doubt.

People wanted explanations. They wanted to understand things for themselves. They wanted more from the priests than disciplinary rules or pious devotions or taboos. They wanted reasons for why they did things. They sought insights and wisdom of their own. They began to search for meaning where, the priestly caste had told them, no one not initiated into priestly rituals could ever go.

With the rise of large cities, personal questions became public questions, and public answers affected individuals everywhere. Why they did what they did became the issues of the day. Questions about what they should do for the making of human community as communities themselves enlarged, became paramount. Why they did things the way they did became the ground of public order. Who knew what kinds of things and who could do what in the public arena — and why — came suddenly and stubbornly into question.

The foment became widespread, touching every class, challenging every old idea. India at 5000 B.C.E. — like Europe at the time of the Reformation, like Bohemian Paris in the 1920s, like Christianity after Vatican II, but thousands of years before them — began to seethe. Things were stirring. Change was on the way.

For centuries, sacred rituals and holy people — the Brahmans, the highest of the Hindu castes — had been sole owners and interpreters of the Vedas, the holy texts of Hinduism. They had determined their meaning and handed down their taboos. They had orchestrated the rituals. They had held the keys to the spiritual kingdom of a people and culture already thousands of years old.

Then, with the rise of population centers, the questions began to ferment in a stew of widespread social unrest. The fermentation began to simmer. People started to question aloud what had been: the answers they'd been given, the rituals they were performing, the religion they had practiced.

Ritual, rather than wisdom, dominated the spiritual scene at this time. Its extravagances and complexities, drained of spiritual impact and more and more remote from the people whose souls it was meant to enliven, lost its power to inspire. It gave form to the spiritual life, but it no longer gave feeling. Most of all, it had become devoid of meaning. It simply failed to bring philosophical substance to the great questions of life.

But the people wanted more than the practices, the hymns, the chants, the superstructure of religion. They wanted to know its mysteries. Where did life come from? What was its source? What did it mean to be human? What was its end? Religion became a question of meaning, of soul.

People began to think for themselves, to ask questions, to experiment with answers. Most of all, they began to cross social boundaries to seek explanations they could not otherwise find. People who had never thought much about life, about creation, about the gods, became restless. People who were not expected to think for themselves — public servants, laborers, students, women — people who had no access to the formal spiritual training of the Brahmans and for centuries had simply accepted the direction of the Brahmans — began to seek out teachers for themselves.

Suddenly, in what had been a highly formalized society, the "Forest Universities" or ashrams — places where spiritual teachers made themselves available to the public at large — became common. Students chose teachers, gurus, to lead them in the spiritual life, to show them the way to wholeness and holiness, to help them discipline their bodies and expand their souls.

And then and there, slowly but surely, out of social upheaval and intellectual unrest, the *Upanishads* — the wisdom literature learned at the feet of a spiritual teacher, the literature that would become the capstone of the *Vedas* — were born. It is out of these dialogues between sage and seeker that the essence of Hindu philosophy, the core of Hindu teachings about life, emerged to shine light on the mysteries of life yet today.

It is in the dialogues of the *Upanishads* and the Indian folklore that these ideas are translated into the stuff of life. It's here that we get a glimpse of the Hindu value system, the Hindu perspective on life, the Hindu belief system that the *Vedas* enshrine. Hindus held dear the notion of the Trinitarian God, the Brahman, which created life, preserved it, and destroyed evil. Most of all, they knew that all living things are Brahman and that Enlightenment is the process of coming to know that.

They live conscious of the law of karma, that good begets good and bad begets bad. Every thought, word, and action has consequences, the Hindu knows, and life goes on and on, one cycle after another, until a person's karma is such that they are reborn into a higher level of spiritual personhood, into Nirvana, the release of the gradually perfecting soul in freedom from the otherwise endless cycle of rebirths.

Salvation, they came to understand, is the result of living out one's duties, of coming to realize one's identity with Brahman, of devotion to the gods through worship, ritual, and pilgrimage.

It is, in short, a lifestyle bent on becoming one with the force of the universe that is Brahman.

It is in the *Upanishads,* therefore, that we begin to understand the power of the personal interaction between the seeker who poses the questions and the teacher who provokes the answer in us. For we are all seeking; we are all full of questions that no amount of rules and rituals can possibly answer but that, we hope, can be unveiled in the life and understanding of another.

The *Upanishads,* one of the most ancient pieces of human religious literature, do not turn us outward in awe of miracles or nature or deity; they turn us inward to seek within the self those divine impulses that lead us, in the end, to a final immersion into Ultimate Mystery, into Brahman.

It is here, too, then, that we may well find some of our own answers to the questions implied in my mail, the questions that, if we live life consciously, if we live life honestly, plague all of us still.

CHAPTER 27

Buddhist Enlightenment and Desirelessness

Finding our way through the dark and rocky parts of life is the very art of living. But if that is the case, the Buddhist tradition may be a more dedicated artist of it than any other. Buddhism commits us to learning to deal with suffering long before suffering ever happens to us.

Suffering, we learn, is part of life — not because it exists outside ourselves somewhere, in the hands of a vindictive God or a pool of evil, for instance, but because we manufacture it for ourselves.

Not unlike ourselves, Gautama Siddhartha, later known as the Buddha, the Enlightened One, once confronted with pain, sought to discover both the source of it and the solution to it. The story of Siddhartha's spiritual development is a fascinating one in an age steeped in its own definitions of the good life.

Siddhartha, born in Nepal in 563 B.C.E., had it all. He lived in one world — powerful, sumptuous, secure — safe from the world outside his father's kingly gates, certain of his own privilege, and destined for inherited power. But then he began to make small forays beyond the walls that separated him and his princely life in a palace from the life of the streets, the villages, the underlings — the mass of humanity.

On his first trip outside the gates, he saw an old man, wrinkled and bent over and slow, his hair white, his strength gone, his body shriveled. Then, on a second trip, he saw a sick man, diminished by disease, writhing in pain, breathing with difficulty. On his third excursion outside the palace compound, he rode by a corpse on the road, blackened, dry, and abandoned. Clearly, life was not unending joy, sumptuous wealth, and perfect security, as his own situation had led him to believe. Other people, the mass of people, were barely grappling themselves through life, one day at a time, every day fraught with some kind of danger for them. Suffering was the lot of life: sickness, diminishment, and death were its hallmarks.

The young man had it all: courtiers and gold, the promise of power, and plenty of pleasures. Since birth he had been promised even more to come: world kingship, unending obeisance from many, conquests without end. But now, he knew in an instant that none of those things was any kind of solution to what he had just seen. Age, disease, and the grave would, in the end, erode them all. Whatever people managed to amass would be diminished by their diminishment. Death would destroy them all. So what was the use of life to begin with?

Gautama Siddhartha, Hindu by birth, found himself in a Hindu culture in a period of great intellectual uneasiness. The old answers simply did not fit anymore; new questions cried out for attention. How did we know that the sacrifices were really effective? Were the gods themselves truly powerful? Was the social order with all its castes and hierarchical overlays actually predetermined? What was the purpose of life? What made a life good? And how could you do anything else in life unless you had some answers to these things?

Siddhartha did what many had been doing before him: he rode off into the forest where seekers and sages of all stripes and social backgrounds had begun to gather to think these things through. It was an age of relentless asceticism as seekers strove to strip themselves of the nonessentials of life in search of the essential. Tired of the pomp and complexity of Hindu sacrifices and rituals, they struggled to become more than what they saw in the culture around them.

Not surprisingly, then, Siddhartha first became a hermit. But simply living alone in the woods did not teach him much about the fullness of life. It simply left him with all his questions, even more starkly than before.

When that did little or nothing to help him understand the nature of life, he became a disciple, putting himself under the teachings of others.

But programs and disciplines and prayers did little to help him transcend what, by then, he knew to be life's great questions. No new answers came, only an increasing awareness that practice alone was an insufficient answer to the prevailing questions of life.

Finally, he tried asceticism. He fasted almost to the point of death before he realized that he had spent more time thinking about asceticism than he had about life. It was then that Gautama became the Buddha, the Enlightened One. It was then he saw into the center of life and came back to tell the rest of us what we had missed. All of life is suffering, he taught. It is suffering that we must learn to transcend.

To do that, he counseled, we must come to grips with the fact that all things are impermanent — all things. Clinging to anything only insures that we will suffer from it.

Everything changes, and so everything must be held with open hands lest it stick to our souls like cement, weigh us down, and bow our souls.

Everything changes and cannot be made captive to a self that is also changing regularly. Totally without independent substance, completely interdependent on everything else that is, the self is at best an illusion, and self-centeredness — the attempt to make ourselves the wholly satisfied center of the world we create — is the greatest mirage of them all.

Desire, he insisted, is simply the seed of our own destruction.

Liberation from suffering depends on desiring nothing, on living well, on coming to realize that life is in the immediate and for the making. It is not a matter of looking for a system, a teacher, answers outside ourselves. It is a matter of coming to control the illusion of the self. "If you meet the Buddha on the road," the Buddha said, "kill him. . . . Be lamps unto yourselves."

India at that time was awash in a religious climate given to complex rituals, a priestly class, and 330 million gods. It had sacred texts and a strictly ordered social system that anointed some with power and privilege, controverted the value of others, denied the merit of many, and came armed with thousands of years of tradition. Clearly, the whole panoply of what we now call Buddhist values and insights unleashed on the religious scene of India a totally heterodox worldview. Without any of those things, this was a new way of being in the world, a new way of being human, a new way of being holy. And people recognized it.

Unlike Hinduism, which had come to be seen by many as endless condemnation to a cycle of endless attempts to achieve an unattainable perfection in birth after birth after birth, here was one who taught the way to the end of suffering. People followed him in adoring crowds both day and night.

The Buddha taught for almost fifty years, walking from one end of India to the other, giving sermons, founding monasteries, challenging the society to simplicity, compassion, acceptance, selflessness, and the character of true happiness.

Today, around the world, Buddhism is expressed in many forms, many ethnic qualities, many classes, and many practices, but the four insights that guide it are its steady foundation everywhere:

1. All of life is suffering.
2. The cause of suffering is selfish craving.
3. Desire can be overcome.
4. The way out of captivity to the self is through the Eightfold Path.

Buddhism is not about beliefs or creeds or gods or rule books or rituals. It is about coming to understand the emptiness of the self. It is a discipline of right views, right desires, right speech, right actions, right livelihood, right effort, right mindfulness, and right concentration or meditation. Buddhism is designed to "blow out the desires" that rage within so we can be free of the emotions they kindle and the pain they bring.

I can be free of myself, Buddhism teaches. I can unbind myself from all that holds me back, straps me down, takes me off my path, and gives me pain. It is only a matter of learning what it is to live in the present, free from concern for either the past or the future. It is about coming to the Eternal Now and doing it right.

If Hinduism was complex, Buddhism was overwhelmingly simple. Hinduism pursued every philosophical idea to its ultimate atomization. Buddhism rested in the surety of one concept alone: suffering is self-made. Perhaps that is precisely why both have so much to teach us, to show us, to make us think newly about again.

CHAPTER 28

Judaism: Community of Justice and Joy

If there's any people on earth who thirst for justice and consciously seek joy, it is surely the Jewish community. And why not? There is hardly a people on earth, after all, who have known more injustice, more harassment, less tolerance, or as much uncertainty. What explains these people? How is it that so small a community has been able to survive such pressure and remain a people?

Hinduism, with its 330 million gods, saw god-ness everywhere, in everything. In it, a person spends one lifetime after another, if necessary, coming to spiritual fulfillment, freeing the spiritual self from the material self. Buddhism, on the other hand, spends little time, if any, talking about God at all. Whatever God is, the Buddha decided, suffering is of our own making and so is our liberation from it.

But for Judaism, God is both the question and the answer.

God, the Jewish people came to understand, was One. It was an understanding of cataclysmic proportions. This God was, indeed, then, all-mighty. But the best news of all was not so much that God was one as it was that this One God was good. The God of the Jews did not torment people, did not abuse them, did not compete with other gods for praise or satisfaction. This God did not trifle with human beings like insects on a pin. This Creator God, who had "led them out of the land of Egypt" and made a people out of them, wished them "well and not woe." This God was a mother, a father, a rock.

For the Jews, God was not many, not evil, not remote. God was not simply *in* history in some stumbling, frightening way. On the contrary, God, personal and beneficent, purposeful and bountiful, mysterious but meaningful, *was* their history — past, present, and to come.

God and the Jewish people, Judaism knew, were linked together in a common human undertaking: to remind the world forever that the One God had created the entire human family and that this God constituted both the destiny of humankind and the way to its fullness.

The way, however, depended on both the achievement of righteousness and the understanding of what characterized real joy.

For Israel, therefore, three elements dominated the life of the Jewish community: Torah, worship, and deeds of loving kindness.

Life became an exercise in coming to know the mind of God. It was also, then, a training ground in the 613 laws or mitzvot that made the will of God real. Torah study, constant reflection on the ways of God with humankind, and constant application of the Word of the God of history to the circumstances of the time became the Jewish passion. This God was not stone; this creation was not static; this Word was not dead.

The five books of the Torah made the relationship between Judaism and its God exceedingly clear. It reminded the Jewish community over and over again: God created us (Genesis), freed us (Exodus), guides us (Leviticus), increases us (Numbers), and is with us (Deuteronomy). This was an eternal relationship — the link between now and eternity — not to be bartered, not to be forgotten, not to be doubted, not to be minimized.

All of life, then, becomes centered on the fine art of balancing the self against the community, the self against the ideals of the God of life. The training starts young, and the scope of it is total. Rabbi Yisrael Deren of Chabad-Lubavitch describes this immersion in ritual and its deep and meaningful symbolism within Jewish tradition. "The haircutting (of a child) itself becomes an educational experience," explains Rabbi Deren. "It's a mitzvah where you cut the hair and you leave the peyot, the hair along the side. And the central message here is that every aspect and every element of our lives ultimately can be endowed, and therefore must be endowed, with a higher and divine purpose — so that even a haircut acquires a religious significance."

Every act of life, then, has to do with the pursuit of right relationships — with God, with the other, with the world. It is a life of total awareness, of complete God-consciousness. But it is not a God-consciousness that is self-centered. It is the spirituality of a people. It is not a God-and-I spirituality. It is a God-and-we relationship.

Just as God cares for the human community, the Jew must also be dedicated to caring for the world. No wonder, then, that such commitment to justice finds its acme in "deeds of loving kindness" that make life on earth what God wants for us all. "Deeds of loving kindness" remind us of God's will for the world.

But the Jewish community, exiled, left without a land, subject to pogroms and holocaust, to temporary refuge and historical rejection, early on lost the notion that God could be confined to sacred places and became witnesses to the notion of sacred time. Sabbath, the promise of God's peace, the experience, however fleeting, of God's rest from tension and struggle, became the center of Jewish life, the hope of the Jewish soul.

Celebration of the Sabbath became a taste of the sweet joy to come, the promise of hope in the future despite the struggles of the present. The God who had brought the Jewish community from one move to another in history, will, the Jew knows, bring them through this dark night, too, to the dawn of peace and wholeness. This tiny respite from personal enslavement, from public oppression, from internal struggle, promises that, little by little, Shabbat will surely come forever, will surely come for us all.

Torah study, acts of loving kindness, and Sabbath give the Jew a vision of life in which God is both the beginning, the present, and the end. It is a life short on theology and long on the practice of living the life God wants for us, long on the practice of life with God. It is life with a God who, the Mishna teaches, says, "Better that the Jews leave me and keep my ways than that they believe in me and stop fulfilling the commandments." Torah, the law that teaches us how we must live, the Jew knows, is the life that leads to God.

But if that is the case, what else is there to be concerned about on this earth that could possibly be greater than Torah study, worship, and deeds of loving kindness?

CHAPTER 29

Christianity: The Call to the Beatitudes

I was studying Hebrew at the local temple when it happened. After weeks of reading Hebrew sentences out loud, stumbling over unfamiliar sounds and guessing at vowels, the little class of five Jews and one Christian — a nun of all things, me — the trust level in the room had risen perceptibly since the first night of the course. "May I ask you a personal question?" one of the women asked. "Why don't you Catholics just admit that you're another type of Jew?" I smiled for a moment. "I'd have no problem with that at all," I answered.

The truth is that the question said a lot about the relationship between us. There is no doubt that Christianity was born in the heart of Judaism. The Jewish prophets are the prophets of Christians, as well. The Jewish scripture, the Hebrew Bible, is part of the Christian holy literature, too. Jesus, the Christ, was Jesus the Jew to the end. Jesus did not start a new religion. That came much later.

Jesus was a Jew whose way of seeing the world drew substantially from the Torah, the Prophets, and the Psalms in which he had been raised and which, as the Evangelists point out, he practiced to the end. He never rejected Judaism — "I have not come to change the law but to complete it," he said quite clearly. "I have not changed one jot or tittle of the law," he said in another place. On the contrary.

Into this environment, Jesus came preaching the God of peace and the

God of love — the God of all creation — as had the great prophets before him. He made no distinctions between peoples — "male or female, Jew or Greek, slave or free," as Paul, the first-century Christian missionary, put it. And, true to the tradition, Jesus insisted that the purity laws — the holiness code — be understood to be always in the service of love, human dignity, and equality.

Jesus took the scriptures and intensified them in order to expose the heart of them. To those who heard, "you shall not murder," he commanded, "love your enemy." To those who heard, "you shall not commit adultery," he said, "You shall not covet, even in your heart."

To Jesus, God was "abba" — father — as the prophet Malachi had said before him, "Have we not all one father?" Clearly, God was not simply lawgiver. Those whom God created, Jesus argued, God loved. All of them. Equally. Whatever their affiliations — Romans and Samaritans, Canaanites as well as Israelites.

He consorted with tax collectors, the very agents of the Roman oppression of the Hebrew people. He dined with the rich, spoke to women, blessed foreigners, consorted with prostitutes, and had a motley band of disciples that included levites, fishermen, tax collectors, even women.

In a world made up of hierarchies and hierarchs, of emperors and serfs, Jesus was the great leveler of society. He became indeed "savior," "liberator," "redeemer" — in ways no one could have imagined. And the people followed him in droves, this pied piper of a renewed humanity, this prophet of a loving God.

Over time, the following of Jesus spawned a world religion that challenges those who make themselves God to remember the mind of God for the world. He preaches a godliness that turns the ways of the world upside down.

In the Beatitudes, the definition of those whose lives are really blessed, really godly, really happy, Jesus calls each and all of us to be a blessing to the world. He brings us beyond and above the motives that drive a world bent on power and greed, on profit and control. Instead, he draws for us a template of godly happiness that is based on humility, compassion, justice, mercy, singleness of heart, peacemaking, and the willingness to pour ourselves out, to spend ourselves to make it all happen.

Blessed are the poor in spirit, he taught. Blessed are those who mourn, those who are meek and humble of heart, those who hunger and thirst for the sake of justice, those who are merciful, pure of heart, peacemakers. And blessed are those who are persecuted for the sake of justice. And he was.

He was a worry to those who saw their social order being undermined, of course, but more than that, he was an irritant to the Romans who feared a promised messianic revolt. In the end, Jesus, the holy one, was "crucified, died, was buried" only to rise again in the hearts and lives and spirits of those who heard his message and waited for his promise to come.

These called themselves "Christians," those who believed that the messiah had already come and left them with the work of bringing to completion the coming reign of God.

This spirituality of equality, love, and universal blessedness stands out to this day as a sign of hope in the God who wishes us all "well and not woe," both in this world and in the next. It is the task of the Christian to love.

CHAPTER 30

Islam: Community of Witness and Submission

From the time a reflective young man struggled in the Arabian Desert in 610 C.E. to hear and to understand, to preach and to proclaim the word of God, Muslims have known themselves to be called first and foremost to submit to the will of God. "Islam," in fact, means "submission." But why?

The city of Mecca in Saudi Arabia in the late sixth century C.E. was a teeming area of transient traders and rival Arab tribes. Whatever its isolation by Western standards of that period, Mecca was a polyglot world of traveling foreigners who plied up and down the routes of caravanserai to sell spices from one area, silks from another, crafts from a world that stretched from the Gulf of Aden to the Mediterranean. It is into this cauldron of commerce, beliefs, gods, and kinship systems that Muhammad ibn Abdallah was born in the clan of Hashim.

Most people of his time and area would have predicted that his biography would be short, or, if not short, at least insignificant. Muhammad, orphaned at an early age, went from one kin to another. First, his grandfather undertook the child's care. Then, when the grandfather died, an uncle took him in. Not surprisingly, he had no special formation whatsoever. He was uneducated, illiterate, and poor.

He didn't have much. But one thing he did have. He had character. He was, those who knew him in those younger days said, honest and just, fair and responsible.

Eventually, Muhammad himself became a trader — a good one — in a culture of traders and nomads. He married Khadija, the older business-woman who owned the caravan he managed, and settled down to a basi-cally unremarkable life.

But there was something else about Muhammad that marked him out. He was a reflective young man who took to making regular retreats into the desert to pray. It was in the desert that, wrapped in prayer, he first heard the voice that said to him, "Recite."

For twenty-two years, Muhammad heard and memorized the words of God that eventually became the Qur'an as we know it today. They con-sumed him for the rest of his life. In the end, the life of Muhammad is the history of a person seized by God.

Muhammad shared his revelations, tentatively and quietly at first, only with his family and immediate circle of friends. Then, little by little, his cir-cle became a community of believers, all witnessing to the fact of the One God in an area that had been host to many people of many different gods. Mecca had become a common shrine for all of them. The Ka'aba, which ironically, tradition said, had been a shrine built by Abraham, had become a mélange of gods meant to welcome every trader who came to town. If anything, Muhammad was not good public relations for a commercial community that clearly boasted its openness to religious impulses of all kinds from all places and clearly profited from that openness economi-cally.

So fraught with tension did the revelations and Muhammad's call to universal conversion become, as a result, that Muhammad finally left Mecca for the exile that turned into empire. Medina became the first of many Islamic communities, organized around Muhammad, the Messen-ger, the Prophet. It allowed itself to be governed according to the principles being revealed to him in the Qur'an, the *Recitation*, which were, he taught, to become the scaffolding of a whole new way of being, not just for Mecca but for the rest of the world as well.

Muhammad, "the seal of the Prophets," the last and final word of God in a tradition that traced itself back to Abraham and forward to Jesus, pro-claimed his revelations as the completion of the Word of God given before him to "the People of the Book," Jews and Christians alike. Islam, the final

Word of God, Muhammad taught, came to correct the corruptions and misunderstandings of the two earlier revelations.

In Islam, an entire way of life as well as a process of personal morality came into being. To be Muslim, to be a follower of Islam, meant to live according to the will of God. It meant to submit all of life, every smallest part of it, in accordance with the principles and practices revealed by the Prophet in the Qur'an.

The Qur'an was the Revelation. Muhammad was its guide. The Qur'an itself and the practice of the community led by Muhammad became the poles between which the Muslim seeks to shape life and attitudes. It is a community of values, a community of tradition, a community of great personal responsibility.

The Qur'an, Islam teaches, answers all the questions of life. Therefore, it was not revealed at once because it was meant to provide a template for all of life's possibilities at all stages. It literally unfolds the various circumstances of all of life so that we are never without a guide to what it means to live in accordance with the will of God.

Islam is deceptively simple and profoundly complex at the same time. It teaches an uncompromising monotheism common, as well, to the People of the Book but more stark in its focus, more encompassing in its unrelenting search for the will of God. Islam struggles. Islam strives. Islam requires effort, *jihad*, at all times. And most of all, perhaps, it places the responsibility for discovering the will of God directly on the shoulders of the individuals. Every Muslim must struggle to determine which of two principles applies to any and every action, which of two practices is best at any given time, which of two responses is the really holy one here and now.

Muhammad and the life of the community he modeled for the rest of us for all time are a guide, yes. But in the end, it is conscious choice, personal choice, that counts, not rote, not rules, not simple ritualistic adherence to someone else's mechanical set of rules.

Islam lays down the non-negotiables and then structures itself to keep them. The holy teachings are so stark, so simple, they can hardly be ignored for want of either awareness or understanding: there is only one God; human beings must submit to the will of God in everything; there will be a Day of Judgment; there is a heaven and a hell; every minute we are all closer to one or the other of them.

And the path is as simple and as clear as the teachings: the Muslim must confess at all times and in all circumstances that "there is only one God, and Muhammad is his prophet."

After that, there is nothing more to say, there is nothing else to do but to live out the submission to the one God that has been proclaimed and to do it according to the Prophet's Recital of the Word of God and the model of his life. Then, to stay on the way, to keep the memory fresh, to remember the uncompromising call of the Qur'an, the Muslim must pray five times a day, fast during the month of Ramadan, give a percentage of all income in alms, and, if possible, make the Haj or the journey to Mecca, the center and heart of Islam.

Islam is, then, about unquestioning faith, immersion in God, care for the other, discipline of the self, and commitment to the tradition.

It is a simplicity of focus that demands a community to live it fully. Islam is not only a faith; it is a way of life, a continual struggle to know the will of God and to live it. It is the relentless pursuit of the will of God. Islam sets out to be the community of God on earth and struggles with every breath of every day to be it.